Better Homes & Gardens.

CHRISTMAS COOKING
FROM THE HEART™

Celebrate the Season

Meredith Consumer Marketing
Des Moines, Iowa

CHRISTMAS COOKING
FROM THE HEART™

MEREDITH CORPORATION CONSUMER MARKETING
Consumer Marketing Product Director: Daniel Fagan
Consumer Marketing Product Manager: Max Daily
Consumer Products Marketing Manager: Kylie Dazzo
Senior Production Manager: Liza Ward

WATERBURY PUBLICATIONS, INC.
Editorial Director: Lisa Kingsley
Creative Director: Ken Carlson
Associate Editor: Tricia Bergman
Associate Design Director: Doug Samuelson
Assistant Editor: Will Bortz
Production Assistant: Mindy Samuelson
Contributing Copy Editor: Peg Smith
Contributing Proofreader: Terri Fredrickson
Contributing Food Stylist: Jennifer Peterson

BETTER HOMES & GARDENS **® MAGAZINE**
Editor in Chief: Stephen Orr
Creative Director: Jennifer D. Madara
Executive Editor: Oma Blaise Ford

MEREDITH CORPORATION
President and CEO: Tom Harty
Chairman: Stephen M. Lacy
Vice Chairman: Mell Meredith Frazier

Our seal assures you that every recipe in *Christmas Cooking from the Heart™* has been tested in the *Better Homes & Gardens*® Test Kitchen. This means that each recipe is practical and reliable and it meets our high standards of taste appeal. We guarantee your satisfaction with this book for as long as you own it.

All of us at Meredith Consumer Marketing are dedicated to providing you with information and ideas to enhance your home. We welcome your comments and suggestions. Write to us at: Meredith Consumer Marketing, 1716 Locust St, Des Moines, IA 50309-3023. *Christmas Cooking from the Heart™* is available by mail. To order editions from past years, call 800/627-5490.

Cover: Triple-Layer Hazelnut Spice Cake (recipe, page 78)

APPLE CINNAMON
BREAD, PAGE 127

SUGAR COOKIES,
PAGE 104

Table of Contents

Celebrate the Season

Food is central to celebrations large and small, and each holiday has distinctive dishes and flavored tastes to commemorate special occasions. Whether you entertain at holiday gatherings, serve houseguests, or bake cookies and breads for neighbors, dependable and delicious recipes are a must.

Better Homes & Gardens® Christmas Cooking from the Heart™ promises delicious recipes that you can rely on—recipes to turn to again and again. Get inspired to bake with intriguing recipes for sweet treats: Macadamia-Cranberry Jumbles (page 96), Caramel-Coconut Cookie Bars (page 111), and Ginger Linzer Cookies (page 107). For holiday brunches, treat family or guests to Sheet Pan Greens and Feta Frittata (page 44), Cranberry Pull-Apart Coffee Cake (page 51), and Citrus Mock Mimosas (page 56).

For sparkling end-of-year festivities, select small bites with big flavor: Sicilian Potato Croquettes (page 130), Caramelized Spicy Roasted Red Pepper Artichoke Dip (page 140), and Apple-Brown Butter Bars (page 143).

Happy Cooking! Happy Holidays!

CARAMEL-COCONUT
COOKIE BARS,
PAGE 111

SPICE-ROASTED
VEGETABLES,
PAGE 14

Gather

Host a dinner party. You decide the size, then select
from main-dish, side, bread, and dessert recipes to
keep guests happy.

STUFFED
SPIRAL HAM,
PAGE 13

FLASH-ROASTED TURKEY

PREP 25 minutes
ROAST 2 hours at 450°F
STAND 30 minutes
COOK 20 minutes

2   large cloves garlic, minced
1   tsp. kosher salt
¾   cup unsalted butter, softened
¼   cup chopped fresh herbs, such as sage, parsley, thyme, and chives
½   tsp. freshly ground black pepper
5   Tbsp. all-purpose flour
1   10- to 12-lb. turkey
    Salt and black pepper
3   large onions
1   large carrot, peeled and quartered
1   stalk celery, quartered
1   bouquet garni (3 sprigs parsley, 3 sprigs thyme, and 1 bay leaf tied into a bundle with 100%-cotton kitchen string)
2   cups dry white wine

1. Preheat oven to 450°F. Place rack in lower third of oven. In a small bowl mash garlic with kosher salt to make a paste. Add butter, herbs, and pepper; mash with a fork. Put one-third of herb butter in a separate bowl; stir in flour. Cover and chill.
2. Remove neck and giblets from turkey; set aside. Discard liver. Pat turkey dry. Working from large cavity end, use your fingers to gently loosen breast skin and leg skin nearest breast. Push remaining butter mixture under loosened skin. Massage to spread butter evenly. Season cavity with salt and pepper. Cut two of the onions into four wedges; finely chop remaining onion. Place four onion wedges in turkey cavity. Season outside of turkey with salt and pepper. Fold neck skin under body, tuck wing tips under breast, and tie drumsticks together with 100% cotton kitchen string.
3. Place turkey on rack in roasting pan; pour 2 cups water into pan. Tent turkey with foil. Roast 2 hours or until an instant-read thermometer inserted in thigh registers 175°F, rotating pan and adding 1 cup water to pan after 1 hour. Remove from oven. Carefully tilt turkey so juices inside turkey run into pan. Discard onion from cavity. Transfer turkey to a platter; loosely cover with foil. Let stand 30 minutes. Remove and discard string.
4. While turkey roasts, for stock, place neck and giblets in a large saucepan. Add remaining four onion wedges, carrot, celery, and bouquet garni to saucepan; fill with cold water (about 4 cups). Bring to boiling, skim foam from surface; reduce heat. Simmer, covered, 1 hour. Strain, discarding solids. Measure 3 cups.
5. For gravy, strain pan juices through a fine-mesh sieve into bowl. Let stand 5 minutes; skim off and reserve fat. Place roasting pan across two burners. Cook chopped onion in ¼ cup reserved fat over medium heat 5 minutes or until golden, stirring and scraping up browned bits. Add wine; bring to boiling. Boil gently 8 to 12 minutes or until liquid is almost evaporated. Add turkey stock and pan juices; bring to boiling. Whisk chilled herb butter into boiling liquid until thickened. Simmer, uncovered, 5 minutes, whisking occasionally. Season with salt and pepper. Slice turkey; serve with gravy. Makes 10 servings.
Tip If desired, place several halved onions or shallots and lemons in a shallow baking pan. Drizzle with olive oil. Roast, uncovered, 30 minutes or until browned and tender. Place around turkey to serve along with fresh sage sprigs to serve.
PER SERVING *634 cal., 31 g fat (13 g sat. fat), 267 mg chol., 706 mg sodium, 7 g carb., 0 g fiber, 71 g pro.*

TOMATO AND ONION BRISKET

PREP 15 minutes
COOK 15 minutes
BAKE 3 hours 10 minutes at 325°F
STAND 15 minutes

1   3½- to 4-lb. fresh beef brisket, trimmed of all but ¼-inch fat
    Kosher salt and freshly ground black pepper
2   Tbsp. olive oil
4   cups chopped onions
1   head garlic, broken into cloves, peeled, and halved
1   celery heart, halved lengthwise
4   fresh bay leaves
1   14.5-oz can diced tomatoes (undrained)
1   cup chicken stock or reduced-sodium chicken broth
1   cup dry white wine
1   Tbsp. tomato paste
    Fresh parsley, torn
    Finely grated fresh horseradish
1   recipe Ginger Pickled Onions

1. Preheat oven to 325°F. Season beef with salt and pepper. Heat oil in a 12-inch skillet over medium-high. Add meat and brown well on both sides; transfer to a 3-qt. baking dish or nonreactive roasting pan. Add onions and garlic to skillet. Cook and stir 5 minutes or until onions are translucent. Stir in celery heart, bay leaves, tomatoes, stock, wine, and tomato paste. Bring to boiling; boil gently, uncovered, 2 to 3 minutes. Pour mixture around meat in dish. Cover with parchment paper, then cover tightly with a double thickness of foil. Bake 3 to 3½ hours or until meat is tender. Transfer meat to a cutting board. Cover and let stand 15 minutes.
2. For sauce, skim fat from cooking liquid. Discard bay leaves. Bake, uncovered, 10 to 15 minutes or until desired consistency. Slice meat across the grain. Serve with sauce; top with parsley and horseradish. Serve with Ginger Pickled Onions. Makes 10 servings.
Ginger Pickled Onions In a nonreactive saucepan combine 1 cup vinegar, ¾ cup packed light brown sugar, 1 tsp. kosher salt, and one 1½-inch piece fresh ginger, peeled and sliced ¼ inch thick. Bring to a rapid simmer, stirring occasionally until sugar is dissolved. Simmer, uncovered, 5 to 7 minutes or until syrupy. Add onion rings and simmer 1 minute more. Remove from heat and cool completely.
PER SERVING *583 cal., 36 g fat (13 g sat. fat), 107 mg chol., 514 mg sodium, 30 g carb., 3 g fiber, 29 g pro.*

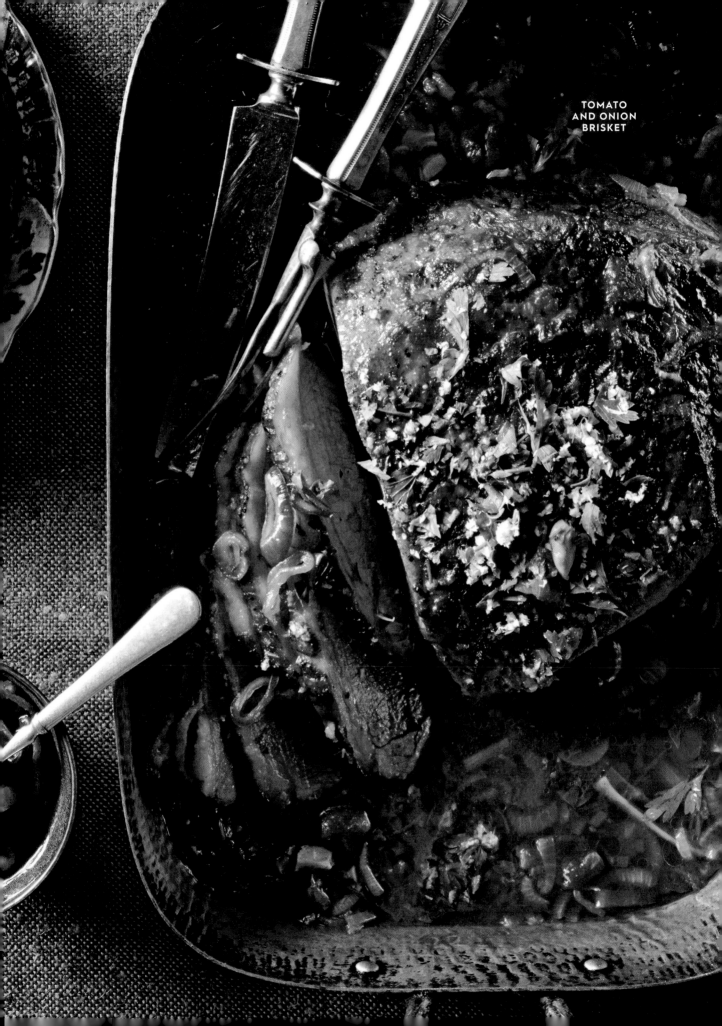

STUFFED
SPIRAL HAM

STUFFED SPIRAL HAM

PREP 20 minutes
BAKE 2 hours at 325°F

1   apple, cored, halved, and thinly sliced
1   pear, cored, halved, and thinly sliced
1   8- to 10-lb. spiral cut ham
4   cloves garlic, sliced
6   sprigs fresh rosemary and/or thyme, cut up
1   recipe Cherry-Rosemary or Honey-Mustard Glaze Clementines (optional)

1. Preheat oven to 325°F. Line a shallow roasting pan with foil. Arrange apple and pear slices between each ham slice, going all the way around the ham. Insert garlic and herb sprigs among slices. Transfer ham, flat side down, to prepared pan. Cover with foil.
2. Bake 2 hours or until browned and heated through (145°F), uncovering and spooning desired glaze over ham the last 45 minutes. Use two large wide spatulas to transfer ham to a platter. Spoon some pan juices over ham. If desired, garnish with clementines and additional herbs. Makes 16 servings.
PER SERVING *178 cal., 4 g fat (1 g sat. fat), 98 mg chol., 1,978 mg sodium, 4 g carb., 0 g fiber, 32 g pro.*
Cherry-Rosemary Glaze In a small bowl stir together ½ cup cherry jam, ¼ cup orange juice, and 1 Tbsp. chopped fresh rosemary.
PER SERVING *40 cal., 0 g fat, 0 mg chol., 4 mg sodium, 10 g carb., 0 g fiber, 0 g pro.*
Honey-Mustard Glaze In a small bowl stir together ½ cup stone-ground mustard, ¼ cup honey, 1 Tbsp. fresh thyme leaves, and ½ tsp. ground cardamom.
PER SERVING *22 cal., 0 g fat, 0 mg chol., 130 mg sodium, 6 g carb., 0 g fiber, 0 g pro.*

BRAISED MAPLE-GLAZED CARROTS

START TO FINISH 30 minutes

2   Tbsp. unsalted butter
2   garlic cloves, halved
1   fresh rosemary sprig
2   lb. carrots, peeled and diagonally sliced ¼ inch thick

BRAISED MAPLE-GLAZED CARROTS

Kosher salt and black pepper
½   cup water
3   Tbsp. orange juice
1   Tbsp. pure maple syrup
1   tsp. Dijon mustard
    Dash cayenne pepper
1   tsp. slivered orange zest*

1. In a large skillet melt butter over medium. Add garlic cloves, cut sides down, and rosemary sprig. Cook until fragrant and garlic begins to brown, 1 to 2 minutes. Remove and discard garlic.
2. Add carrots to skillet. Season with salt and black pepper. Add water. Bring just to boiling; reduce heat. Simmer, covered, 8 to 10 minutes or until carrots are almost tender.
3. Remove and discard rosemary sprig. Add juice, maple syrup, mustard, and cayenne pepper to carrots; increase heat to medium-high. Cook 5 minutes, stirring frequently, until liquid is syrupy and carrots are lightly glazed. Transfer to a serving bowl; sprinkle with slivered orange zest. Makes 6 servings.
*Tip To sliver zest, peel wide strips of orange zest using a vegetable peeler then cut into thin slivers.
PER SERVING *108 cal., 4 g fat (2 g sat. fat), 10 mg chol., 171 mg sodium, 18 g carb., 4 g fiber, 2 g pro.*

SPICE-ROASTED VEGETABLES

PREP 30 minutes
ROAST 40 minutes at 425°F

1½ tsp. coriander seeds
1 tsp. cumin seeds
½ tsp. caraway seeds
¼ cup olive oil
½ tsp. sweet paprika
4 to 4½ lb. mixed vegetables (such as small leeks, halved lengthwise and rinsed; small beets, peeled, and quartered; carrots, peeled; shishito peppers; small or regular eggplant, cut into eighths)
Salt and black pepper
Flowers from nasturtiums and/or signet or calendula marigolds (optional)

1. Preheat oven to 425°F. In a small skillet heat coriander, cumin, and caraway seeds over low 2 minutes or just until fragrant, shaking pan occasionally. Remove from heat and cool slightly. Transfer to a spice grinder and grind to a powder (or use a mortar and pestle). Combine with olive oil and paprika. Place vegetables in an extra-large shallow baking pan and toss with seasoning. Sprinkle with salt and pepper.
2. Roast 40 minutes or until vegetables are tender and charred, turning once or twice. If desired, top with flowers. Makes 6 servings.
*Tip If using red beets, dress separately with oil mixture and place in a separate baking pan to prevent bleeding onto other vegetables. If using eggplant, add to baking pan the last 30 minutes of roasting.
PER SERVING *214 cal., 10 g fat (1 g sat. fat), 0 mg chol., 132 mg sodium, 31 g carb., 8 g fiber, 4 g pro.*

BRAISED COLLARD GREENS WITH BACON

PREP 30 minutes
COOK 40 minutes

3 slices bacon, cut crosswise into 1-inch pieces
½ cup chopped onion
4 cloves garlic, minced
6 cups thinly sliced, stemmed collard greens
1 14.5-oz. can chicken broth
1 tsp. sugar
¼ tsp. salt
⅛ tsp. cayenne pepper
1 15-oz. can black-eyed peas, rinsed and drained (optional)
2 Tbsp. cider vinegar

1. In a 10-inch cast-iron skillet cook bacon over medium until crisp. Drain on paper towels, reserving 2 Tbsp. drippings in skillet.
2. Add onion to reserved drippings; cook 5 minutes or until softened. Add garlic; cook and stir 3 minutes. Add collard greens, half at a time, stirring until wilted after each addition. Add broth, sugar, salt, and cayenne pepper.
3. Bring to boiling; reduce heat. Simmer, covered, 30 to 45 minutes or until greens are tender, stirring occasionally. Stir in black-eyed peas (if using) and vinegar; heat through. Top with bacon. Makes 6 servings.
PER SERVING *98 cal., 6 g fat (2 g sat. fat), 17 mg chol., 631 mg sodium, 5 g carb., 1 g fiber, 5 g pro.*

SPICE-ROASTED VEGETABLES

BRAISED COLLARD
GREENS WITH BACON

MASHED ROOT VEGETABLES WITH PARMESAN

ASIAN-STYLE SWEET POTATOES

MASHED ROOT VEGETABLES WITH PARMESAN

PREP 25 minutes
COOK 20 minutes
BAKE 15 minutes at 400°F
BROIL 2 minutes

3   lb. assorted root vegetables, such as carrots, parsnips, turnips, rutabaga, and/or red or yellow potatoes
3   cloves garlic, peeled
½   tsp. salt
¼   cup milk
1   Tbsp. olive oil
1   Tbsp. butter
¼   tsp. black pepper
¼   cup snipped fresh parsley
½   cup shredded Parmesan cheese (2 oz.)

1. Preheat oven to 400°F. Peel root vegetables; cut vegetables into 2- to 3-inch pieces. Place vegetables, garlic, and ¼ tsp. of the salt in a large saucepan; add enough cold water to cover. Bring to boiling; reduce heat.

Simmer, covered, 20 minutes or until tender. Meanwhile, in a small saucepan heat milk, olive oil, and butter until butter is melted.

2. Drain vegetables; return to pan. Mash vegetables. Stir milk mixture, remaining ¼ tsp. salt, and pepper into vegetables. Stir in half the parsley and half the cheese. Spread mashed vegetables in a 1½-qt. gratin dish. Top with remaining cheese.

3. Bake, uncovered, 15 minutes or until cheese is melted and vegetables are heated through. If desired, preheat broiler; broil vegetables 4 to 5 inches from heat 2 minutes or until top is browned. Top with remaining parsley. Makes 8 servings.

Make Ahead Prepare as directed through Step 2, except cool mashed vegetables slightly before topping with Parmesan. Cover and chill up to 24 hours. Uncover; bake in a preheated 400°F oven 30 minutes or until heated through. Continue as directed.

PER SERVING *81 cal., 5 g fat (2 g sat. fat), 8 mg chol., 260 mg sodium, 8 g carb., 1 g fiber, 3 g pro.*

ASIAN-STYLE SWEET POTATOES

PREP 20 minutes
ROAST 25 minutes at 425°F

2   to 2½ lb. sweet potatoes, peeled and cut into ½- to ¾-inch cubes (6 cups)
1   large onion, halved and sliced (1½ cups)
3   Tbsp. vegetable oil
½   tsp. salt
¼   tsp. black pepper
3   cups broccoli florets
⅓   cup water
⅓   cup almond butter
3   Tbsp. lemon juice
3   Tbsp. soy sauce
1   Tbsp. minced garlic
1   Tbsp. grated fresh ginger
¼   tsp. crushed red pepper
¼   cup unsweetened flaked coconut, toasted (tip, page 96)
¼   cup chopped almonds or pecans, toasted (tip, page 22)

1. Preheat oven to 425°F. In a large bowl combine sweet potatoes, onion,

MUSTARD-DRESSED
ROASTED
VEGETABLES WITH
CRANBERRIES

oil, salt, and pepper; toss to coat. Divide mixture among two 15×10-inch baking pans. Roast, uncovered, on two separate racks, 15 minutes. Add broccoli to pans. Roast 10 minutes more or until vegetables are browned and tender.

2. Meanwhile, for dressing, in a small bowl whisk together water, almond butter, lemon juice, soy sauce, garlic, ginger, and crushed red pepper until smooth.

3. Transfer vegetable mixture to a platter. Drizzle with dressing. Sprinkle with coconut and nuts. Makes 6 servings.

PER SERVING *345 cal., 19 g fat (3 g sat. fat), 0 mg chol., 812 mg sodium, 39 g carb., 8 g fiber, 9 g pro.*

MUSTARD-DRESSED ROASTED VEGETABLES WITH CRANBERRIES

PREP 15 minutes
ROAST 25 minutes at 425°F

1	lb. sweet potatoes, peeled
12	oz. fresh green beans, trimmed
4	Tbsp. olive oil
½	tsp. kosher salt
	Freshly ground black pepper
1	Tbsp. balsamic vinegar
2	tsp. whole grain mustard
1	clove garlic, minced
¼	cup dried cranberries
½	tsp. dried rosemary, crushed or 1 tsp. snipped fresh rosemary

1. Preheat oven to 425°F. Halve sweet potatoes lengthwise; slice into ½-inch half-moons. In a 15×10-inch baking pan toss potatoes with beans, 2 Tbsp. olive oil, ¼ tsp. kosher salt, and pepper to taste. Roast 20 minutes, stirring once. For vinaigrette, in a bowl whisk together vinegar, mustard, garlic, remaining oil and salt, and pepper to taste.

2. Remove from oven; stir in cranberries and rosemary. Return to oven; roast 5 minutes more. Toss vegetables with vinaigrette. Serve warm or at room temperature. Makes 4 servings.

PER SERVING *272 cal., 14 g fat (2 g sat. fat), 0 mg chol., 242 mg sodium, 36 g carb., 6 g fiber, 3 g pro.*

ORANGE SQUASH

PUMPKIN-PARMESAN RISOTTO

PREP 20 minutes
COOK 25 minutes

- 3 Tbsp. unsalted butter
- 1 cup finely chopped onion
- 1 clove garlic, minced
- 2 cups uncooked Arborio rice
- 1 cup dry white wine
- 1½ Tbsp. snipped fresh sage
- 2 to 2½ cups water
- 1¾ cups chicken broth
- 1 cup canned pumpkin
- 2 oz. Parmigiano-Reggiano cheese, finely shredded (½ cup)
  Parmigiano-Reggiano cheese, shaved (optional)
  Fresh sage leaves (optional)

1. In a heavy 4-qt. saucepan heat butter over medium until melted. Add onion and garlic; cook 3 minutes or until tender, stirring occasionally. Add rice; cook and stir 2 minutes. Carefully add wine; cook and stir until liquid is absorbed. Stir in snipped sage.
2. Meanwhile, in a large saucepan bring water and broth to boiling; reduce heat to simmer. Slowly add 1 cup broth mixture to rice mixture, stirring constantly. Cook and stir over medium until most of the liquid is absorbed. Add another 1 cup broth mixture, stirring constantly. Cook and stir until most liquid is absorbed. Add enough remaining broth mixture, 1 cup at a time, cooking and stirring just until rice is tender but firm and risotto is creamy.
3. Stir in pumpkin and shredded cheese. Cook 1 minute or until heated through, stirring occasionally. If desired, top servings with shaved cheese and sage leaves. Makes 4 servings.
PER SERVING *385 cal., 12 g fat (7 g sat. fat), 26 mg chol., 547 mg sodium, 61 g carb., 6 g fiber, 10 g pro.*

ORANGE SQUASH

START TO FINISH 30 minutes

- 1 2- to 2½-lb. butternut squash, peeled
  Kosher salt and freshly ground black pepper
- 2 Tbsp. vegetable oil, plus more as needed
- ½ cup vegetable broth
- ½ cup orange juice
- 4 cloves garlic, minced
- 2 Tbsp. butter
- 1 Tbsp. chopped fresh sage

1. Cut squash neck into ½-inch thick slices. Halve remaining squash and remove seeds and strings. Slice ½ inch thick. Season generously with salt and pepper. Heat a heavy 12-inch skillet over medium-high. Remove skillet from heat; add oil. Swirl to coat bottom of skillet. Return to medium-high. Add half the squash (don't crowd pan). Cook 2½ to 3 minutes or until a crust forms. Turn and cook 4 to 5 minutes more or until squash is crusted and tender, reducing heat to medium, if necessary, to prevent overbrowning.
2. Transfer squash to a serving platter; cover loosely to keep warm. Repeat with remaining squash, adding oil if needed. Remove skillet from heat. For sauce, carefully add broth, juice, and garlic. Bring to boiling, stirring to scrape up browned bits. Boil gently, uncovered, 5 minutes or until reduced by about half. Remove from heat. Stir in butter and sage.
3. Spoon sauce over squash. Top with additional sage if desired. Makes 4 servings.
PER SERVING *218 cal., 13 g fat (4 g sat. fat), 15 mg chol., 276 mg sodium, 27 g carb., 4 g fiber, 2 g pro.*

PUMPKIN-PARMESAN RISOTTO

WINTER GREENS AND BROCCOLINI TART

PREP 25 minutes
BAKE 5 minutes at 450°F
COOK 11 minutes

1   recipe No-Fail Tart Crust
3   to 4 Tbsp. Sesame Spice Mix
¾   cup purchased hummus
¼   cup olive oil
1   lemon, sliced and seeded
8   oz. Broccolini or broccoli
    florets, trimmed, and stems split
    lengthwise
½   cup water
3   oz. Lacinato kale leaves, stems
    removed (about half a bunch)
½   tsp. kosher salt

1. Prepare No-Fail Tart Crust as directed. After trimming, sprinkle dough with 2 Tbsp. Sesame Spice Mix; press into crust.
2. Increase oven temperature to 450°F. Spread hummus on baked crust. Drizzle 1 Tbsp. olive oil on hummus. In a 12-inch skillet heat 1 Tbsp. olive oil over medium-high. Add lemon slices. Cook 2 minutes on each side or until browned. Remove; set aside. Add Broccolini and water to skillet. Cook 5 to 7 minutes or until Broccolini is almost tender, stirring occasionally. Place kale leaves on Broccolini during last 2 minutes of cooking to lightly steam. Remove Broccolini and kale from skillet; toss with 1 Tbsp. olive oil. Sprinkle with salt.
3. Arrange Broccolini, kale, and lemon slices on tart. Bake 5 minutes. Drizzle with remaining 1 Tbsp. olive oil; sprinkle with 1 to 2 Tbsp. Sesame Spice Mix. Makes 12 servings.

No-Fail Tart Crust Preheat oven to 450°F. In a food processor pulse 1¾ cups flour; ½ cup butter, cubed; and ½ tsp. salt until mixture resembles fine crumbs. In a small bowl whisk together two egg yolks and 3 Tbsp. water. With processor running, add yolk mixture and process just until dough starts to come together, about 5 seconds. Gather dough into a ball; slightly flatten and roll out between two pieces of parchment paper into a 12×9-inch rectangle. Transfer dough to pan. Press into corners; trim excess. Using a fork, prick dough all over. Line pastry with a double thickness of foil. Bake 12 minutes.

WINTER GREENS AND BROCCOLINI TART

Reduce temperature to 350°F. Remove foil. Bake 8 minutes or until pastry is golden. Cool completely.
Sesame Spice Mix Heat a small skillet over medium heat. Add 2 Tbsp. sesame seeds, 1 Tbsp. coriander seeds, and 1 Tbsp. cumin seeds. Cook and stir until lightly toasted, 2 to 3 minutes. Using a spice grinder, coarsely grind toasted sesame seeds, coriander, and cumin together. Add ¼ cup roasted salted sunflower kernels to grinder and pulse once. Stir in ½ tsp. crushed red pepper. Store in a cool dark place in an airtight container up to 1 month.
PER SERVING *348 cal., 23 g fat (9 g sat. fat), 77 mg chol., 390 mg sodium, 31 g carb., 4 g fiber, 7 g pro.*

CRUNCHY KALE SALAD
WITH CREAMY TOMATO-
GARLIC DRESSING

CRUNCHY KALE SALAD WITH CREAMY TOMATO-GARLIC DRESSING

PREP 20 minutes
ROAST 25 minutes at 425°F

1 recipe Creamy Tomato-Garlic Dressing
6 cups torn, trimmed fresh kale
2 tsp. olive oil
¼ tsp. salt
1 cup bite-size red, yellow, and/or orange bell pepper strips
6 tsp. slivered almonds, toasted (tip, page 220 and chopped

1. Prepare Creamy Tomato-Garlic Dressing. For salad, in a large bowl combine kale, olive oil, and salt. Using clean hands gently rub oil and salt into kale for 2 minutes or until kale is softened and volume is nearly half.
2. Divide salad among serving plates. Top with bell pepper and almonds. Drizzle each salad with 1 Tbsp. dressing. (Refrigerate remaining dressing in an airtight container up to 1 week.) Makes 6 servings.

Creamy Tomato-Garlic Dressing
Preheat oven to 425°F. Cut off the top ¼ inch of one garlic bulb to expose individual cloves. Remove any loose, papery outer layers. Place bulb, cut side up, in a custard cup or on a double thickness of foil. Drizzle bulb with ½ tsp. of the olive oil. Cover with foil or bring up foil around bulb and fold edges together to loosely enclose. Roast 25 to 35 minutes or until garlic feels soft when squeezed. Cool until easy to handle. Meanwhile, in a bowl combine ¼ cup boiling water and 3 Tbsp. snipped dried tomatoes (not oil-packed). Cover and let stand 10 minutes. Pour undrained tomatoes into a blender. Squeeze garlic cloves and add to blender. Add remaining 2½ tsp. olive oil, ⅔ cup buttermilk, 1 tsp. lemon zest, 2 Tbsp. lemon juice, ⅛ tsp. salt, and ⅛ tsp. black pepper. Cover and blend until smooth. Makes about 1¼ cups dressing.
PER SERVING *80 cal., 4 g fat (1 g sat. fat), 0 mg chol., 148 mg sodium, 9 g carb., 2 g fiber, 4 g pro.*

FIG AND WALNUT WILD RICE DRESSING

FIG AND WALNUT WILD RICE DRESSING

PREP 15 minutes
COOK 40 minutes
BAKE 35 minutes at 350°F

Nonstick cooking spray
3 cups reduced-sodium chicken broth or vegetable broth
¾ cup wild rice
¾ cup brown rice
3 Tbsp. olive oil
2 cups finely chopped yellow onion
1 cup finely chopped celery
¼ tsp. ground nutmeg
¼ tsp. ground white or black pepper
¾ cup chopped fresh parsley
½ cup walnuts, chopped and toasted (tip, page 22)
¼ cup chopped dried Mission figs
¼ cup chopped fresh sage or 1½ tsp. dried sage, crushed

1. Preheat oven to 350°F. Coat a 2-qt. baking dish with cooking spray.
2. In a 3-qt. saucepan combine broth, wild rice, and brown rice. Bring to boiling; reduce heat. Simmer, covered, 40 to 45 minutes or until rice is tender.
3. Meanwhile, in a 10-inch skillet heat oil over medium. Add onion, celery, nutmeg, and pepper; cook 10 minutes or until tender. Transfer to a large bowl. Stir in remaining ingredients.
4. Drain rice, reserving cooking liquid. Add rice to bowl. Measure 1 cup cooking liquid (if necessary, add broth or water to equal 1 cup); stir into rice mixture. Transfer to prepared baking dish; cover with foil.
5. Bake 25 minutes. Uncover; bake 10 minutes more or until heated through. Makes 8 servings.
PER SERVING *240 cal., 11 g fat (1 g sat. fat), 0 mg chol., 40 mg sodium, 31 g carb., 3 g fiber, 6 g pro.*

APPLE, CELERY ROOT, AND FENNEL SALAD

START TO FINISH 45 minutes

¼ cup walnut oil or sunflower oil
2 Tbsp. cider vinegar
1 Tbsp. lemon juice
1 small shallot, finely chopped
1 tsp. honey mustard
¼ tsp. salt
¼ tsp. black pepper
4 cups torn curly endive
1 head butterhead (Boston) lettuce, torn
1 medium red apple, cored and cut into matchstick-size pieces
1 small celery root, peeled and cut into matchstick-size pieces
1 small fennel bulb, trimmed, halved, and thinly sliced
2 oz. blue cheese or feta cheese, shredded*
⅓ cup chopped walnuts, toasted**

1. For the dressing, in a screw-top jar combine oil, cider vinegar, lemon juice, shallot, honey mustard, salt, and pepper. Cover and shake well.

2. In a large bowl combine endive and butterhead lettuce. Add three-fourths of the dressing; toss to coat. Divide greens among salad plates.

3. In the same bowl combine apple, celery root, and fennel. Toss with remaining dressing to coat. Top greens with apple mixture. Top salads with blue cheese and walnuts. Makes 6 servings.

*Tip To grate blue cheese or feta cheese, purchase a whole wedge and freeze 30 minutes before grating.

**Tip Toast small amounts of nuts and seeds in a dry skillet over medium heat 3 to 5 minutes, stirring frequently. For larger amounts, preheat oven to 350°F. Spread nuts or seeds in a shallow baking pan. Bake 5 to 10 minutes or until lightly browned, shaking pan once or twice.

PER SERVING *210 cal., 16 g fat (3 g sat. fat), 7 mg chol., 299 mg sodium, 13 g carb., 3 g fiber, 5 g pro.*

APPLE, CELERY ROOT, AND FENNEL SALAD

BEET SALAD WITH GOAT CHEESE AND WALNUTS

PREP 20 minutes

2 5-oz. pkg. spring mix salad greens
½ cup balsamic vinaigrette
20 to 24 oz. cooked beets, chopped
⅓ cup snipped fresh parsley
1 tsp. freshly ground black pepper
⅓ cup coarsely chopped walnuts, toasted (tip, page 22)
5 oz. goat cheese (chèvre), crumbled

1. Arrange greens on a serving platter; drizzle with ¼ cup vinaigrette.
2. In a bowl combine beets, parsley, and pepper. Drizzle with remaining vinaigrette; toss to coat. Spoon beet mixture onto greens; sprinkle with walnuts and goat cheese. Makes 6 servings.
PER SERVING *160 cal., 10 g fat (3 g sat. fat), 7 mg chol., 700 mg sodium, 14 g carb., 3 g fiber, 6 g pro.*

LENTIL SOUP WITH LEMON AND DILL

PREP 20 minutes
COOK 25 minutes

1 Tbsp. extra virgin olive oil
1 tsp. cumin seeds
1 32-oz. box vegetable stock
2 cups water
1½ cups French green lentils, rinsed and drained
1½ cups chopped carrots
2 cloves garlic, minced
1 bay leaf
½ tsp. kosher salt
3 Tbsp. lemon juice
¼ tsp. black pepper
  Plain yogurt
½ cup lightly packed fresh dill sprigs, coarsely chopped
¼ cup finely chopped green onions

1. In a large saucepan heat oil over medium-high. Add cumin seeds; cook 30 seconds or until toasted. Stir in the next seven ingredients (through salt). Bring to boiling; reduce heat. Simmer, covered, 25 minutes or until lentils are tender. Discard bay leaf. Add lemon juice and pepper. Serve with yogurt, dill, and green onions. Makes 4 servings.
PER SERVING *346 cal., 5 g fat (1 g sat. fat), 2 mg chol., 858 mg sodium, 56 g carb., 9 g fiber, 20 g pro.*

BEET SALAD WITH GOAT CHEESE AND WALNUTS

LENTIL SOUP WITH LEMON AND DILL

CHICKPEA, LEEK, AND SPINACH SOUP

START TO FINISH 25 minutes

2   Tbsp. extra virgin olive oil
2   medium leeks, white and light green parts only, thinly sliced, washed, and drained
2   15- to 16-oz. cans chickpeas, rinsed and drained
2   cloves garlic, thinly sliced
4   cups reduced-sodium chicken or vegetable stock or broth
1   cup water
1   lemon, juiced (3 Tbsp.)
2   5-oz. pkg. baby spinach
1   Tbsp. fresh thyme, chopped
     Kosher salt
     Freshly ground black pepper

1. In a 4-qt. pot heat oil over medium; add leeks. Cook, stirring occasionally, 5 to 7 minutes or until tender but not browned. Stir in chickpeas and garlic. Cook 2 minutes, stirring occasionally.
2. Add stock and water. Bring to boiling. Reduce heat. Add lemon juice. Simmer, uncovered, 5 minutes. Gradually stir in the spinach and thyme. Cook 1 minute or until spinach is wilted. Season to taste with salt and pepper. Makes 8 servings.
PER SERVING *132 cal., 5 g fat (0 g sat. fat), 0 mg chol., 428 mg sodium, 17 g carb., 5 g fiber, 7 g pro.*

CHICKPEA, LEEK, AND SPINACH SOUP

VEGGIE SKILLET BISCUITS

PREP 25 minutes
BAKE 15 minutes at 450°F

1   small stalk broccoli, stem peeled and shredded and florets broken apart
¾   cup shredded zucchini
⅓   cup shredded carrot
2¼   cups all-purpose flour
2   tsp. baking powder
1   tsp. salt
½   tsp. baking soda
½   tsp. black pepper
½   cup unsalted butter, cut up
⅔   cup shredded extra-sharp cheddar cheese
1   cup plain whole milk Greek yogurt
1   Tbsp. unsalted butter, melted
     Sea salt flakes

1. Preheat oven to 450°F. Coarsely chop broccoli florets and shredded broccoli, zucchini, and carrot (2 cups total). Transfer vegetables to a medium bowl. Sprinkle with ¼ cup flour; toss to coat.
2. In a large bowl stir together remaining 2 cups flour, baking powder, salt, baking soda, and pepper. Using a pastry blender, cut in ½ cup butter until mixture resembles coarse crumbs. Fold in vegetable mixture and cheese. Stir in yogurt until dough is moistened. Gently knead in bowl just until dough comes together.
3. Turn dough out onto a lightly floured surface. Pat dough to 1¼-inch thickness. Cut with a floured 2½-inch biscuit cutter or glass. Repeat with scraps, dipping cutter into flour between cuts.
4. Place biscuits in a 12-inch cast-iron skillet. Bake 15 to 18 minutes or until golden. Brush with melted butter and sprinkle with sea salt. Serve warm. Makes 9 servings.
PER SERVING *281 cal., 16 g fat (10 g sat. fat), 42 mg chol., 440 mg sodium, 27 g carb., 1 g fiber, 8 g pro.*

CRANBERRY CHUTNEY

START TO FINISH 30 minutes

1   navel orange
¾   cup packed brown sugar
¼   cup cider vinegar
¼   cup water
⅓   cup finely chopped red onion
4   ¼-inch slices fresh ginger

VEGGIE
SKILLET
BISCUITS

1   tsp. mustard seeds
¼   tsp. salt
⅛   tsp. crushed red pepper
1   12-oz. pkg. cranberries, rinsed
1   Granny Smith apple, peeled and
    chopped

1. Remove 2 tsp. zest from orange; set aside. Cut ¼ inch off top and bottom of orange. With a sharp knife, remove skin and white membrane. Working over a medium saucepan (to catch juice), separate orange segments Cut segments into small pieces; set aside. Squeeze remaining membrane over pan to extract any remaining juice.
2. Add brown sugar, vinegar, water, onion, ginger, mustard seeds, salt, and crushed red pepper to juice in saucepan. Bring to boiling over medium-high. Add cranberries and orange zest. Return to boiling; reduce heat. Cook, uncovered, 7 minutes,

stirring occasionally. Add apple and cook 3 minutes more or just until apple is tender.
3. Remove from heat; remove and discard ginger and stir in reserved orange segments. Serve warm or cover and refrigerate up to 2 days. Bring to room temperature before serving. Makes 6 servings.
PER SERVING *163 cal., 0 fat, 0 mg chol., 107 mg sodium, 41 g carb., 4 g fiber, 1 g pro.*

BACON-SHISHITO RELISH

START TO FINISH 20 minutes

3   slices bacon
½   cup finely chopped red onion
6   oz. shishito peppers, stemmed and
    chopped
2   Tbsp. red wine vinegar

1   cup cherry tomatoes, quartered
2   Tbsp. chopped fresh parsley
    Salt and black pepper

1. In a large skillet cook bacon until crisp. Transfer to paper towels, reserving drippings in skillet. Crumble bacon.
2. Add onion to skillet. Cook and stir over medium heat 4 minutes or until tender. Add shishito peppers. Cook 4 minutes or until browned, stirring occasionally. Stir in vinegar, scraping up any browned bits. Cook, uncovered, 30 seconds. Remove from heat. Stir in bacon, cherry tomatoes, and parsley. Season with salt and black pepper. Chill, covered, up to 3 days. Makes 10 servings.
PER SERVING *45 cal., 2 g fat (1 g sat. fat), 6 mg chol., 128 mg sodium, 3 g carb., 1 g fiber, 2 g pro.*

BACON-CHEDDAR
POTATO DIP,
PAGE 37

Celebration
Appetizers

Set out a buffet of nibbles and festive drinks for
guests as they mix and mingle. Keep it simple with
two or three appetizers, or present an assortment

BUFFALO CHICKEN
SLIDERS, PAGE 31

27

CUBAN
DRUMMIES

CUBAN DRUMMIES

PREP 20 minutes
MARINATE 2 hours
BAKE 25 minutes at 450°F

12 chicken wings (about 2 lb.)*
1   cup mango nectar
½   cup lemon juice
½   cup orange juice
½   cup snipped fresh Italian parsley
¼   cup red wine vinegar
¼   cup olive oil
1   to 2 fresh jalapeños,** seeded and finely chopped
6   cloves garlic, minced
1   tsp. salt
½   tsp. ground cumin
1   mango, seeded, peeled, and chopped
⅓   cup chopped onion (1 small)
¼   cup snipped fresh cilantro
    Orange wedges (optional)

1. Cut off and discard tips of chicken wings or reserve to make broth. Cut wings at joints for 24 pieces. Place chicken in a resealable plastic bag set in a shallow dish.
2. For marinade, in a medium bowl whisk together mango nectar, lemon juice, orange juice, parsley, vinegar, oil, jalapeño, garlic, salt, and cumin. Remove ½ cup marinade for sauce; cover and chill until needed.
3. Pour remaining marinade over chicken. Seal bag; turn to coat chicken. Marinate in refrigerator 2 to 24 hours, turning bag occasionally.
4. Preheat oven to 450°F. Drain chicken,;discard marinade. Arrange chicken in a single layer on unheated rack of large broiler pan. Bake 25 minutes or until chicken is golden brown, turning once.
5. Meanwhile, for sauce, in a blender combine reserved ½ cup marinade, mango, onion, and cilantro. Cover and blend until smooth. Serve chicken with sauce and, if desired, orange wedges. Makes 12 servings.
*Tip Or use 24 chicken wing drumettes.
**Tip Chile peppers contain oils that can irritate skin and eyes. Wear plastic or rubber gloves when working with them.
PER SERVING *278 cal., 20 g fat (4 g sat. fat), 97 mg chol., 283 mg sodium, 9 g carb., 1 g fiber, 17 g pro.*

OVEN-BAKED SICILIAN MEATBALLS

OVEN-BAKED SICILIAN MEATBALLS

PREP 25 minutes
BAKE 25 minutes at 350°F

⅔   cup soft bread crumbs
3   Tbsp. milk
1   egg, lightly beaten
⅓   cup grated Parmesan cheese
¼   cup finely chopped onion
¼   cup snipped fresh basil
3   Tbsp. pine nuts, toasted (tip, page 22)
3   Tbsp. dried currants
½   tsp. salt
1   clove garlic, minced
¼   tsp. freshly ground black pepper
1   lb. bulk sweet Italian sausage
    Pasta sauce, warmed (optional)

1. Preheat oven to 350°F. In a large bowl combine bread crumbs and milk. Let stand 5 minutes. Stir in egg, Parmesan cheese, onion, basil, pine nuts, currants, salt, garlic, and black pepper. Add sausage; mix well.
2. Shape mixture into 24 meatballs. Place in a single layer on a 15×10-inch baking pan. Bake, uncovered, 25 to 30 minutes or until meatballs are done (160°F). Drain off fat. If desired, serve with pasta sauce for dipping. Makes 24 servings.
PER SERVING *58 cal., 3 g fat (1 g sat. fat), 16 mg chol., 199 mg sodium, 3 g carb., 0 g fiber, 4 g pro.*

BACON-WRAPPED
SHRIMP

MANCHEGO-
STUFFED
MUSHROOMS

BACON-WRAPPED SHRIMP

PREP 30 minutes
MARINATE 15 minutes
BROIL 7 minutes

48	peeled and deveined shrimp, tails on if desired
¼	cup dry white wine
1	lemon (2 tsp. zest; 3 Tbsp. juice)
4	tsp. chili garlic sauce
1½	tsp. salt
6	strips bacon
⅔	cup mayonnaise
2	green onions, finely chopped

1. Combine shrimp, wine, lemon zest, 1 tsp. chili garlic sauce, and salt in glass dish; marinate 15 minutes. Remove shrimp; drain on paper towels. Discard marinade.

2. Cut bacon into four pieces; flatten with the back of a knife to prevent curling. Wrap each shrimp in a piece of bacon (neck to tail in a half-moon); secure with a wooden toothpick. Place bacon-wrapped shrimp in a single layer on an unheated rack of a broiler pan.
3. Place oven rack 3 to 4 inches from broiler. Preheat broiler. Broil, turning twice, until shrimp are opaque and bacon is cooked through and crisp, 7 to 9 minutes total.
4. For remoulade, in a small bowl stir together mayonnaise, lemon juice, remaining 1 Tbsp. chili garlic sauce, 1 tsp. salt, and green onions. Cover and chill until serving.
5. Serve shrimp with remoulade for dipping. Makes 12 servings.
PER SERVING *45 cal., 3 g fat (1 g sat. fat), 24 mg chol., 134 mg sodium, 0 g carb., 0 g fiber, 3 g pro.*

MANCHEGO-STUFFED MUSHROOMS

PREP 20 minutes
BAKE 25 minutes at 400°F

½	cup panko
2	oz. Manchego or Parmesan cheese, finely shredded
6	Tbsp. extra virgin olive oil
2	Tbsp. chopped fresh parsley
2	cloves garlic, minced
½	tsp. smoked paprika
¼	tsp salt
1	lb. 2- to 2½-inch button mushrooms (12 to 14), stemmed
¼	cup chopped pitted Castelvetrano olives
3	thin slices Jamón Ibérico or prosciutto, cut into narrow strips

1. Preheat oven to 400°F. Line a 15×10-inch baking pan with parchment paper.

BUFFALO CHICKEN SLIDERS

2. For filling, in a small bowl stir together panko, cheese, 2 Tbsp. of the olive oil, parsley, garlic, paprika, and salt. Spoon filling into mushroom caps, pressing in and mounding filling for full caps. Arrange in prepared pan. Drizzle remaining 4 Tbsp. oil over mushrooms.

3. Bake 25 minutes or until mushrooms are tender and filling is golden. Cool slightly. To serve, top with olives and ham. Makes 12 servings.

PER SERVING *105 cal., 9 g fat (2 g sat. fat), 5 mg chol., 145 mg sodium, 3 g carb., 1 g fiber, 3 g pro.*

BUFFALO CHICKEN SLIDERS

PREP 25 minutes
SLOW COOK 6 hours on low or 3 hours on high

1   Tbsp. vegetable oil
2   to 2½ lb. skinless, boneless chicken thighs or breast halves
1   14.5-oz. can reduced-sodium chicken broth
1   cup sliced celery
1   cup buffalo wing sauce
16   sweet Hawaiian rolls or slider buns, split
     Blue cheese salad dressing
     Carrot and/or celery sticks

1. In an extra-large skillet heat oil over medium-high. Cook chicken, half at a time, 8 minutes or until browned, turning once.

2. Place chicken in a 3½- or 4-qt. slow cooker. Add broth and sliced celery. Cover and cook on low 6 to 7 hours or high 3 to 3½ hours.

3. Remove chicken from cooker. Shred using two forks. Pour cooking liquid into a bowl. Return chicken to cooker. Stir in buffalo wing sauce and, if needed, some of the cooking liquid to moisten.

4. Use a slotted spoon to spoon chicken in rolls. Serve with dressing and carrot and/or celery sticks. Makes 16 servings.

PER SERVING *255 cal., 15 g fat (4 g sat. fat), 57 mg chol., 256 mg sodium, 20 g carb., 1 g fiber, 11 g pro.*

HERBED CHEESE
MINI PEPPERS

HERBED CHEESE MINI PEPPERS

START TO FINISH 25 minutes

- 10 red, yellow, and/or orange miniature sweet peppers
- 1 lemon
- 1 8-oz. pkg. reduced-fat cream cheese (neufchatel), softened
- 1 to 2 Tbsp. chopped fresh oregano, rosemary, tarragon, or thyme; or ½ to 1 tsp. dried oregano, rosemary, tarragon, or thyme, crushed
- 2 Tbsp. finely chopped jalapeño pepper (tip, page 29)
- 1 Tbsp. milk

1. Cut each pepper in half lengthwise; remove seeds. Remove zest and squeeze 1 Tbsp. juice from lemon.
2. In a small bowl combine cream cheese, oregano, jalapeño, milk, and lemon juice. If needed, stir in enough additional milk to reach piping consistency.
3. Pipe or spoon cream cheese filling into pepper halves. Serve immediately or store in refrigerator up to 4 hours. Sprinkle with lemon zest and, if desired, additional fresh oregano. Makes 20 servings.
PER SERVING *36 cal., 3 g fat (1 g sat. fat), 8 mg chol., 39 mg sodium, 2 g carb., 0 g fiber, 1 g pro.*

CHORIZO, KALE, AND SWEET POTATO GALETTE

PREP 40 minutes
RISE 1 hour
BAKE 25 minutes at 425°F
COOL 5 minutes

- 1 recipe Olive Oil Galette Dough
- 2 medium sweet potatoes, peeled and sliced into ¼-inch rounds
- 2 Tbsp. olive oil
- ¼ tsp. salt
- ¼ tsp. black pepper
- 8 oz. bulk mild chorizo
- ½ medium red onion, thinly sliced
- 2 cloves garlic, minced
- 8 oz. Manchego cheese, shredded
- 2 cups lightly packed coarsely chopped kale
- 1½ Tbsp. sherry vinegar
- 1 egg white, lightly beaten
- 1 Tbsp. cornmeal

CHORIZO, KALE, AND SWEET POTATO GALETTE

1. Prepare Olive Oil Galette Dough. Preheat oven to 425°F. In a large bowl combine sweet potato slices and olive oil; toss to coat. Arrange sweet potatoes in a single layer on a large baking sheet. Sprinkle with salt and pepper. Bake 10 minutes or until tender.
3. Meanwhile, in a large skillet cook chorizo, onion, and garlic over medium-high heat 6 to 8 minutes or until chorizo is browned. Drain fat from skillet.
4. On a large sheet of parchment paper, roll dough to a 17×12-inch oval. Slide parchment and pastry onto baking sheet.
5. Sprinkle chorizo mixture on dough, leaving a 2-inch border. Sprinkle with cheese; top with sweet potato slices.
6. In a medium bowl combine kale and sherry vinegar. Toss well to coat kale with vinegar. Sprinkle kale over sweet potatoes. Fold edge of dough over filling, pleating as necessary. Brush dough with egg white; sprinkle lightly with cornmeal.

7. Bake 15 to 20 minutes or until crust is golden and cheese is melted. Cool 5 minutes. Makes 8 servings.
Olive Oil Galette Dough In a small bowl combine ¾ cup water (105°F to 115°F), 1 pkg. active dry yeast, and 1 tsp. sugar. Let stand 5 to 7 minutes or until foamy. Meanwhile, in a large bowl whisk together 1 egg and 1 egg yolk until combined. Whisk in 2 Tbsp. olive oil, 1 tsp. salt, and the yeast mixture. Stir in enough bread flour (2 to 2½ cups) to form a dough. Turn out dough onto a lightly floured surface. Knead in enough bread flour (about ½ cup) to make a soft dough that is smooth and elastic (3 to 5 minutes total). Place dough in a large greased bowl, turning once to grease the surface. Cover and let rise in a warm place until nearly double in size (about 1 hour). Punch down dough.
PER SERVING *540 cal., 31 g fat (13 g sat. fat), 101 mg chol., 1,079 mg sodium, 42 g carb., 3 g fiber, 22 g pro.*

STEAMED
DUMPLINGS

STEAMED DUMPLINGS

PREP 30 minutes
STEAM 10 minutes per batch

1   recipe Cilantro-Lime Chicken
     Filling, Lemon-Basil Veggie Filling,
     or Shrimp Scampi Filling
     Nonstick cooking spray
48   cups dumpling or gyoza wrappers

1. Prepare desired filling; chill. Line the
bottom of a bamboo steamer basket
with a piece of parchment cut to fit.
Using a sharp knife, make several slits in
paper; lightly coat with cooking spray.
2. Spoon 1 Tbsp. filling in center of each
dumpling wrapper. Working around the
dumpling, pull wrapper up over filling,
pleating to enclose filling. Pinch dough
at top then twist.
3. Transfer to prepared steamer basket;
do not crowd dumplings. Repeat with
remaining wrappers and filling. Fill and
shape remaining batches of dumplings
while first batches steam.
4. Set basket over a skillet of boiling
water (not touching water). Cover;
steam 10 minutes or until dumplings
reach 165°F when an instant-read
thermometer is inserted into filling. Serve
with dipping sauce. Makes 48 servings.
Make Ahead Prepare all dumplings
through Step 3. Place in a single layer
on a baking sheet; cover with plastic
wrap. Freeze until firm. Transfer to
airtight containers. Cover;freeze up to
3 months. Steam 12 minutes or until done
(165°F).
Cilantro-Lime Chicken Filling In a
bowl combine 1 lb. ground chicken;
1 poblano chile pepper, stemmed,
seeded, and finely chopped (tip,
page 29); ¼ cup chopped cilantro;
2 Tbsp. lime juice; 2 tsp. ground cumin;
1 tsp. crushed red pepper; 1 tsp. olive
oil; ½ tsp. kosher salt; and ¼ tsp. black
pepper. **For dipping sauce:** In a
small bowl stir together ½ cup canola
oil, ¼ cup lime juice, ½ cup chopped
cilantro, and ¼ tsp. salt.
PER SERVING *67 cal., 4 g fat (0 g sat.
fat), 8 mg chol., 30 mg sodium, 6 g
carb., 0 g fiber, 3 g pro.*
Lemon-Basil Veggie Filling On a bowl
combine 2 medium zucchini, shredded
and squeezed dry; 4 oz. chopped
mushrooms; ¼ cup chopped fresh basil;
2 tsp. lemon zest; 2 Tbsp. lemon juice;
2 cloves garlic, minced; 1 tsp. olive oil;

½ tsp. dried thyme, crushed; ½ tsp. kosher salt; and ¼ tsp. black pepper. **For dipping sauce:** In a small bowl stir together ½ cup canola oil, ½ cup chopped fresh basil, ¼ cup lemon juice, and ¼ tsp. salt.

PER SERVING *55 cal., 1 g pro., 7 g carb., 3 g fat (0 g sat. fat), 0 mg chol., 0 g fiber, 25 mg sodium*

Shrimp Scampi Filling For filling: Combine 1½ lb. medium shrimp in shells, peeled, deveined, and finely chopped; ⅓ cup capers; 2 shallots, finely chopped; 3 Tbsp. chopped fresh parsley; 4 cloves garlic, minced; 1 tsp. olive oil; ½ tsp. kosher salt; and ¼ tsp. black pepper. **For dipping sauce:** In a small bowl stir together ½ cup melted butter, 2 Tbsp. Worcestershire sauce, and two green onions, thinly sliced.

PER SERVING *61 cal., 2 g fat (1 g sat. fat), 25 mg chol., 72 mg sodium, 6 g carb., 0 g fiber, 3 g pro.*

CUCUMBER-FETA DIP

PREP 20 minutes
CHILL 2 hours

1   cup plain Greek yogurt
½   cup light sour cream
½   cup crumbled feta cheese
¼   cup finely chopped red onion
1   Tbsp. lemon juice
½   tsp. salt
2   cups coarsely shredded English cucumber
    Pomegranate seeds (optional)
    Snipped fresh mint leaves (optional)

1. For dip, in a medium bowl combine yogurt, sour cream, feta cheese, onion, lemon juice, and salt. Chill, covered, 2 to 8 hours.
2. Before serving, place shredded cucumber in a fine-mesh sieve. Use the back of a large spoon or a rubber spatula to press cucumber to remove excess liquid. Stir cucumber into dip. If desired, sprinkle with pomegranate seeds and snipped fresh mint. Makes 9 servings.

PER SERVING *68 cal., 4 g fat (3 g sat. fat), 14 mg chol., 239 mg sodium, 4 g carb., 0 g fiber, 4 g pro.*

CHORIZO-POBLANO ARTICHOKE DIP

PREP 30 minutes
BAKE 25 minutes at 425°F/30 minutes at 350°F
STAND 30 minutes

2   fresh poblano peppers (tip, page 29)
2   14-oz. cans artichoke hearts, rinsed and drained
4   oz. bulk uncooked chorizo sausage
1   8-oz. carton sour cream
2   Tbsp. all-purpose flour
½   cup mayonnaise
¾   cup finely shredded Parmesan cheese
¼   cup sliced green onions
¼   cup chopped fresh cilantro

1. Preheat oven to 425°F. To roast peppers, halve peppers lengthwise; remove stems, seeds, and membranes. Place pepper halves, cut sides down, on a foil-lined baking sheet. Roast 25 minutes or until peppers are charred and tender. Wrap peppers in the foil and let stand 15 minutes or until cool enough to handle. Reduce oven temperature to 350°F.
2. Meanwhile, place artichoke hearts in a fine-mesh sieve or colander. To remove excess liquid, firmly press on artichoke hearts with paper towels. Chop artichoke hearts. Set aside. Use a sharp knife to loosen edges of pepper skins; gently pull off skins in strips and discard. Chop roasted peppers.
3. In a large skillet cook chorizo over medium-high heat until browned, stirring to break up meat as it cooks. Using a slotted spoon, transfer to a paper-towel-lined plate.
4. In a large bowl stir together sour cream and flour until combined. Stir in mayonnaise, ½ cup of the cheese, roasted pepper strips, artichokes, chorizo, green onions, and cilantro. Transfer to a 9-inch pie plate. Sprinkle with remaining cheese.
5. Bake, uncovered, 30 minutes or until edges are lightly browned and dip is hot in center. Let stand 15 minutes. Top with additional sliced green onions and cilantro leaves. Makes 16 servings.

PER SERVING *140 cal., 12 g fat (4 g sat. fat), 20 mg chol., 293 mg sodium, 5 g carb., 1 g fiber, 4 g pro.*

CUCUMBER-FETA DIP

CHORIZO-POBLANO ARTICHOKE DIP

ITALIAN SAUSAGE
ARTICHOKE DIP

ITALIAN SAUSAGE ARTICHOKE DIP

PREP 20 minutes
BAKE 30 minutes at 350°F
COOL 15 minutes

- 2   14-oz. cans artichoke hearts, rinsed and drained
- 4   oz. bulk hot Italian sausage
- 1   8-oz. carton sour cream
- 2   Tbsp. all-purpose flour
- ½   cup mayonnaise
- ¾   cup finely shredded Parmesan cheese
- ¼   cup pitted Kalamata olives, coarsely chopped
- 1   cup cherry tomatoes
- 1   Tbsp. olive oil
- ½   tsp. salt
- 2   Tbsp. capers, drained and patted dry

1. Preheat oven to 350°F. Place artichoke hearts in a fine-mesh sieve or colander. To remove excess liquid, press firmly on artichokes with paper towels. Chop artichokes and set aside.
2. In a large skillet cook sausage over medium-high heat until browned. Using a slotted spoon, transfer to a paper-towel-lined plate.
3. In a large bowl stir together sour cream and flour. Stir in mayonnaise, ½ cup of the cheese, olives, artichokes, and sausage. Transfer to a 9-inch pie plate. Sprinkle with remaining cheese.
4. In a shallow baking pan lined with foil, combine cherry tomatoes with olive oil and salt. Bake tomatoes and dip, uncovered, 30 minutes or until dip is heated through and edges are lightly browned, and tomatoes are slightly charred. Cool dip and tomatoes 15 minutes. Top dip with tomatoes and capers. Makes 16 servings.
PER SERVING *141 cal., 13 g fat (4 g sat. fat), 19 mg chol., 332 mg sodium, 4 g carb., 1 g fiber, 3 g pro.*

BACON-CHEDDAR POTATO DIP

PREP 30 minutes
COOK 15 minutes
BAKE 20 minutes at 425°F

- 2¼   lb. Yukon gold or other yellow potatoes, peeled and quartered
- 4   slices hickory- or applewood-smoked bacon

BACON-CHEDDAR POTATO DIP

1 8-oz. container cream cheese spread
1 cup shredded sharp cheddar cheese (4 oz.)
½ cup sour cream
¼ cup chopped green onions
¼ tsp. garlic salt
   Sweet pepper wedges and/or sour cream-and onion-flavor potato chips

1. Preheat oven to 425°F. In a large covered saucepan cook potatoes in enough lightly salted boiling to cover 15 to 20 minutes or until tender; drain.

2. Meanwhile, in a 9-inch cast-iron skillet cook bacon over medium heat until crisp. Drain on paper towels; reserve 1 Tbsp. drippings in skillet. Crumble bacon; set aside 1 Tbsp. for topping.

3. In a large bowl combine remaining crumbled bacon, cream cheese, ¾ cup of the cheddar cheese, sour cream, green onions, and garlic salt. Press cooked potatoes through a ricer onto cheese mixture;* stir to combine.

4. Spoon dip into skillet; spread evenly. Transfer to oven; bake 20 minutes or until heated through.

5. Preheat broiler. Top dip with remaining ¼ cup cheddar cheese and reserved 1 Tbsp. crumbled bacon. Broil 4 to 5 inches from heat 1 to 2 minutes or until cheese is bubbly. Serve with sweet peppers and/or potato chips. Makes 24 servings.

*Tip Or mash potatoes with a potato masher until fluffy.

PER SERVING 94 cal., 6 g fat (3 g sat. fat), 17 mg chol., 108 mg sodium, 8 g carb., 1 g fiber, 3 g pro.

ROOT VEGGIE
CHIPS WITH
SEA SALT

ROOT VEGGIE CHIPS WITH SEA SALT

PREP 20 minutes
DEHYDRATE 8 hours

3   to 4 cups peeled (if desired) and
    thinly sliced sweet potatoes, blue
    potatoes, beets, parsnips, carrots,
    rutabagas, and/or celery roots*
½ tsp. sea salt

1. Bring a large pot of salted water to
boiling over high heat. Add vegetables;**
cook 30 seconds. Drain vegetables in
a colander set in a sink. Rinse with cold
water and drain again; pat dry.
2. Place vegetables in a large bowl
and sprinkle with salt; toss to coat.
Arrange in a single layer on mesh-lined
dehydrator trays.
3. Dehydrate at 135°F for 8 to 10 hours
or until dry and crisp, shifting trays to
dry chips evenly. When done, chips will
be evenly dry, edges will curl, and chips
will be crisp. Continue drying if chips are
not crisp. (Timing may vary depending
on humidity and moisture in vegetables.)
If desired, sprinkle with additional salt
before serving. Makes 6 servings.
***Tip** Use a mandoline to slice
vegetables evenly.
****Tip** If using beets, cook beet slices
separately to prevent them from
staining other vegetables.
PER SERVING *50 cal., 0 fat 0 mg chol.,*
223 mg sodium, 12 g carb., 2 g fiber,
1 g pro.

SWEET AND
SMOKY NUTS

SWEET AND SMOKY NUTS

PREP 15 minutes
BAKE 25 minutes at 350°F

1   egg white
1½ cups dry-roasted peanuts
5½ cups pecan halves, walnut halves,
    whole almonds, and/or hazelnuts
⅓ cup packed brown sugar
2   tsp. smoked paprika
1   tsp. kosher salt
¼ tsp. ground cinnamon
¼ tsp. ground allspice

1. Preheat oven to 350°F. Line a 15×10-inch
baking pan with foil or parchment paper.
2. In a large bowl whisk egg white
until foamy. Add peanuts and nuts;
toss gently to coat. Stir in remaining
ingredients. Spread nuts in prepared
baking pan.
3. Bake 25 to 30 minutes or until nuts are
toasted and dry, stirring twice. Remove
from oven and stir. Cool completely in
pan. Break up any large clusters. Makes
28 servings.
PER SERVING *165 cal., 13 g fat (1 g sat. fat),*
0 mg chol., 126 mg sodium, 9 g carb.,
2 g fiber, 5 g pro.

CLEMENTINE-CRANBERRY MOCKTAIL

START TO FINISH 15 minutes

2   cups cranberry juice, chilled
1   cup clementine juice (from about
    8 clementines)
¾ cup lime juice
3   Tbsp. honey or simple syrup
    Ice cubes
2   cups club soda, chilled
    Sliced clementine, whole cranberries
    and/or superfine sugar (optional)

1. In a pitcher combine cranberry juice,
clementine juice, lime juice, and honey; stir
until honey is dissolved. Cover and chill up
to 24 hours.
2. Just before serving, add ice cubes
and club soda. If desired, rim glass with
superfine sugar or garnish drink with a
slice of clementine or whole cranberries.
Makes 8 servings.
PER SERVING *79 cal., 0 fat, 0 mg chol.,*
22 mg sodium, 21 g carb., 0 g fiber,
0 g pro.

APPLE CIDER BOURBON PUNCH

START TO FINISH 15 minutes

2   Granny Smith apples, cored and cut
    into chunks
2   Tbsp. fresh lemon juice
½ tsp. ground cinnamon
3¾ cups sparkling apple juice, chilled
1½ cups bourbon
1½ cups spiced apple cider, chilled
4   to 5 cups ice cubes

1. In a medium bowl toss apples with
lemon juice and cinnamon.
2. In a large pitcher stir together sparkling
apple juice, bourbon, and spiced cider. To
serve, add ice and apple chunks to each
glass. Pour over punch. Makes 8 servings.
PER SERVING *200 cal., 0 fat, 0 mg chol.,*
17 mg sodium, 26 g carb., 1 g fiber, 0 g pro.

APPLE CIDER
BOURBON PUNCH

Scrumptious Brunch

Rouse sleepyheads with breakfast and brunch aromas. Choose from savory egg dishes, sweet pastries, warm drinks, and refreshing mocktails.

CHIPOTLE CHICKEN QUICHE, PAGE 46

PUMPKIN WAFFLES
WITH MAPLE-
WALNUT CREAM,
PAGE 55

41

CHILAQUILES
BREAKFAST
CASSEROLE

CHILAQUILES BREAKFAST CASSEROLE

PREP 35 minutes
CHILL 8 hours
BAKE 1 hour at 350°F
STAND 10 minutes

- 12 6-inch corn tortillas, quartered
- 1 Tbsp. vegetable oil
- 1 cup chopped onion
- 4 cloves garlic, minced
- 2 tsp. dried oregano, crushed
- 1 28-oz. can crushed tomatoes, undrained
- 1 cup reduced-sodium chicken broth
- 2 chipotle peppers in adobo sauce, finely chopped
- 2 cups shredded cooked chicken
- 8 eggs
- ¼ tsp. black pepper
   Toppings, such as avocado, Cotija or feta cheese, tortilla strips, and/or cilantro

1. Preheat oven to 350°F. Grease a 3-qt. baking dish. Spread tortillas on two baking sheets. Bake on separate oven racks 15 minutes. Remove; cool.
2. Meanwhile, in a large skillet heat oil over medium-high. Add onion, garlic, and oregano. Cook and stir 2 minutes. Add tomatoes, broth, and chipotle peppers. Bring to boiling; reduce heat. Simmer, uncovered, 10 minutes, stirring occasionally. Stir in chicken.
3. Cover bottom of prepared baking dish with tortillas. Top with chicken mixture; let cool. Cover; chill overnight.
4. Preheat oven to 350°F. Bake, covered, 35 minutes. Remove from oven. Make eight indents in casserole with the back of a spoon. Crack an egg into a custard cup; slip egg into each indent. Sprinkle with black pepper. Bake, uncovered, 10 to 15 minutes or until whites are set and yolks are thickened. Remove. Let stand 10 minutes. Serve with desired toppings. Makes 8 servings.
PER SERVING *303 cal., 15 g fat (4 g sat. fat), 225 mg chol., 464 mg sodium, 22 g carb., 4 g fiber, 22 g pro.*

BISCUITS AND GRAVY BREAKFAST CASSEROLE

BISCUITS AND GRAVY BREAKFAST CASSEROLE

PREP 15 minutes
CHILL 2 hours
BAKE 9 minutes at 400°F/50 minutes at 350°F
STAND 10 minutes

- 2 12-oz. tubes refrigerated flaky biscuits, quartered
- 1 lb. bulk pork sausage, browned and drained (2 cups cooked)
- 1 cup shredded white cheddar cheese (4 oz.)
- 8 eggs
- 4 cups milk
- ¼ tsp. black pepper
- 2 Tbsp. butter
- 1 Tbsp. all-purpose flour

1. Preheat oven to 400°F. Spread biscuits in layers on two large baking sheets. Bake 9 to 11 minutes or until golden. Cool on baking sheets on a wire rack.
2. Grease a 3-qt. rectangular baking dish. Place half the biscuit pieces in prepared dish. Top with 1½ cups sausage and half the cheese (cover and chill remaining sausage until needed). Top with remaining biscuits.
3. In a large bowl beat together eggs, 3 cups milk, and ⅛ tsp. pepper. Pour egg mixture over biscuits in dish. Using the back of a spoon, gently press down layers to moisten. Top with remaining cheese. Cover and chill at least 2 hours or overnight.
4. Preheat oven to 350°F. Uncover dish. Bake 50 minutes or until puffed, golden, and set. Cover with foil the last 5 to 10 minutes of baking, if needed to prevent overbrowning. Let stand 10 minutes before serving.
5. Meanwhile, for gravy, in a small saucepan melt butter over medium heat. Whisk in flour and ⅛ tsp. pepper. Whisk in remaining 1 cup milk. Cook and stir until thickened and bubbly. Stir in remaining ½ cup sausage. Cook and stir 1 minute more. Spoon over casserole before serving. Makes 12 servings.
PER SERVING *405 cal., 23 g fat (10 g sat. fat), 173 mg chol., 865 mg sodium, 30 g carb., 1 g fiber, 18 g pro.*

SHEET PAN GREENS AND FETA FRITTATA

PREP 10 minutes
BAKE 35 minutes at 375°F
STAND 10 minutes

Nonstick cooking spray
2   Tbsp. olive oil
1   16-oz. bunch rainbow chard
1   cup cherry tomatoes, halved
1   shallot, thinly sliced
¼   tsp. salt
12 eggs
1   cup milk
4   oz. feta cheese, crumbled
¼   tsp. black pepper
¼   cup grated Parmesan cheese
¼   cup fresh herbs, such as basil, oregano, and/or Italian parsley

1. Preheat oven to 375°F. Coat a 15×10-inch baking pan with nonstick cooking spray. Add 1 Tbsp. of the oil to pan. Place in oven 5 minutes. Meanwhile, remove chard leaves from stems. Chop leaves (about 8 cups). Trim and thinly slice stems (about 2½ cups). Add stems to baking pan. Bake 5 minutes. Add leaves, tomatoes, shallot, remaining oil, and salt. Toss to coat. Roast 10 minutes or until chard is wilted and tomatoes soften, stirring once.

2. Meanwhile, in a large bowl whisk eggs, milk, feta, and pepper. Pour evenly over vegetables. Sprinkle with Parmesan.

3. Bake 20 minutes or until frittata is set. Remove; turn oven to broil. Top frittata with additional tomatoes if desired.

Broil 3 to 5 minutes or until frittata and tomatoes are lightly browned. Top with fresh herbs. Makes 6 servings.

PER SERVING *291 cal., 20 g fat (8 g sat. fat), 395 mg chol., 635 mg sodium, 9 g carb., 2 g fiber, 19 g pro.*

SQUASH, BACON, AND FETA BREAKFAST BAKE

PREP 35 minutes
BAKE 1 hour at 375°F/25 minutes at 350°F

1   3-lb. spaghetti squash
    Nonstick cooking spray
2   eggs, lightly beaten
⅓   cup finely shredded Parmesan cheese
3   Tbsp. all-purpose flour
2   Tbsp. snipped fresh sage
6   slices bacon, coarsely chopped
3   cups coarsely chopped trimmed Swiss chard leaves, kale, and/or spinach
⅓   cup feta cheese, crumbled
6   eggs
¼   tsp. salt
¼   tsp. black pepper

1. Preheat oven to 375°F. Line a small baking pan with parchment paper. Cut squash in half crosswise; remove and discard seeds. Place squash halves, cut sides down, in prepared baking pan. Bake 1 hour or until squash is tender. Cool on a wire rack. Reduce oven temperature to 350°F.

2. Coat a 2-qt. rectangular baking dish with cooking spray. For crust, in a large bowl combine two lightly beaten eggs, Parmesan, flour, and sage. Using a fork, scrape squash pulp into egg mixture; stir gently to combine. Spread mixture in prepared baking dish. Bake 20 minutes or until crust is set and edges start to brown.

3. Meanwhile, in a large nonstick skillet cook bacon over medium heat just until browned but not crisp. Drain bacon on paper towels; discard drippings. Coat skillet with cooking spray. Add Swiss chard; cook and stir 1 minute.

4. Top crust with chard and feta cheese; sprinkle with bacon. Bake 5 minutes or until heated through.

5. Coat the same skillet with cooking spray; heat over medium. Break three eggs into skillet, keeping eggs separate. Sprinkle with ⅛ tsp. each salt and

SHEET PAN GREENS AND FETA FRITTATA

pepper. Reduce heat to low; cook eggs 3 to 4 minutes or until whites are set and yolks start to thicken. Remove from heat for sunny-side-up eggs. For fried eggs over-easy or over-hard, turn eggs and cook 30 seconds more (for over-easy) or 1 minute more (for over-hard). Remove from skillet; keep warm. Repeat with remaining three eggs, salt, and pepper.

6. To serve, cut casserole into six portions; top each with one egg. Makes 6 servings.

PER SERVING *229 cal., 12 g fat (5 g sat. fat), 262 mg chol., 480 mg sodium, 16 g carb., 3 g fiber, 15 g pro.*

OVERNIGHT BREAKFAST PIE

PREP 20 minutes
CHILL 2 hours
BAKE 50 minutes at 325°F

- 8 slices bacon
- ½ cup panko bread crumbs
- 5 eggs
- 2½ cups frozen shredded hash brown potatoes
- 1 cup shredded Swiss cheese (4 oz.)
- ½ cup cottage cheese
- ⅓ cup milk
- ¼ cup chopped green onions (2)
- ½ tsp. salt
- ¼ tsp. black pepper
- 4 drops bottled hot pepper sauce
  Sliced green onions (optional)

1. In a large skillet cook bacon over medium heat until crisp. Drain bacon on paper towels, reserving 1 Tbsp. drippings in skillet. Crumble bacon; set aside. Stir bread crumbs into reserved drippings. Transfer to a small bowl; cover and chill until needed.
2. Lightly grease a 9-inch pie plate. In a bowl beat eggs with a fork until foamy. Stir in crumbled bacon, potatoes, Swiss cheese, cottage cheese, milk, chopped green onions, salt, pepper, and hot pepper sauce. Pour into prepared pie plate. Cover; chill 2 to 24 hours.
3. Preheat oven to 325°F. Sprinkle pie with bread crumb mixture. Bake, uncovered, 50 minutes or until a knife inserted in center comes out clean. If desired, top with sliced green onions. Cut into wedges. Makes 6 servings.
PER SERVING *324 cal., 17 g fat (7 g sat. fat), 210 mg chol., 640 mg sodium, 22 g carb., 2 g fiber, 20 g pro.*

SQUASH, BACON, AND FETA BREAKFAST BAKE

OVERNIGHT BREAKFAST PIE

SPINACH DUTCH BABY

PREP 10 minutes
BAKE 25 minutes at 425°F
STAND 5 minutes

3   Tbsp. olive oil
½   cup all-purpose flour
½   cup milk
3   eggs
½   tsp. salt
½   tsp. freshly ground black pepper
3   cups fresh spinach
½   cup shredded sharp white
      cheddar cheese (2 oz.)
2   cups cherry tomatoes
3   cloves garlic, minced
3   slices bacon, crisp-cooked and
      crumbled

1. Place 2 Tbsp. olive oil in a large skillet; place in a cold oven. Preheat oven to 425°F.
2. In a medium bowl whisk together flour, milk, eggs, salt, and black pepper until smooth. Chop enough spinach to equal ½ cup. Stir into batter. Pour batter into hot skillet. Bake 20 minutes. Sprinkle with cheese. In a baking pan toss tomatoes with olive oil and garlic; add to oven. Bake 5 minutes or until Dutch Baby is puffed and golden and tomatoes are slightly charred. Transfer to a wire rack; let stand 5 minutes. Top with roasted tomatoes, wilted spinach, and crumbled bacon. Makes 4 servings.
PER SERVING *325 cal., 21 g fat (6 g sat. fat), 162 mg chol., 572 mg sodium, 19 g carb., 2 g fiber, 14 g pro.*

HAM AND SWISS WAFFLES WITH MUSTARD SOUR CREAM

PREP 25 minutes
STAND 1 hour 10 minutes
BAKE 2 minutes per batch

1¾   cups warm milk (105°F to 115°F)
1   Tbsp. sugar
1   pkg. active dry yeast
2   eggs, lightly beaten
½   cup butter, melted
2¼   cups all-purpose flour
8   oz. cooked boneless ham, finely
       chopped
1½   cups shredded Swiss cheese (6 oz.)
½   cup sour cream
2   Tbsp. stone-ground mustard
       Honey
       Snipped chives

1. In a small bowl combine ½ cup of the warm milk, the sugar, and yeast. Let stand 10 minutes or until foamy. Meanwhile, in a medium bowl combine eggs, melted butter, and remaining 1¼ cups warm milk.
2. Place flour in a large bowl; make a well in center. Add egg mixture and yeast mixture to flour. Stir just until moistened (batter should be slightly lumpy). Cover with plastic wrap; let stand at room temperature 1 hour. Gently fold in ham and cheese.
3. Add batter to a preheated, well-greased waffle baker according to manufacturer's directions. Close lid quickly; do not open until done. Bake according to manufacturer's directions until golden and crisp, about 2 minutes. When done, use a fork to lift off grid. Keep warm in a 200°F oven while baking remaining waffles.
4. Meanwhile, in a small bowl stir together sour cream and mustard. Top waffles with sour cream mixture, honey, and chives. Makes 8 servings.
PER SERVING *458 cal., 25 g fat (14 g sat. fat), 123 mg chol., 590 mg sodium, 39 g carb., 1 g fiber, 19 g pro.*

SPINACH DUTCH BABY

CHIPOTLE CHICKEN QUICHE

PREP 30 minutes
BAKE 30 minutes at 400°F/1 hour 10 minutes at 325°F
COOL 40 minutes

1   recipe Deep-Dish Pastry Shell
6   eggs
2   cups plain fat-free Greek yogurt
1   cup milk
1   tsp. ground cumin
1   tsp. chili powder
½   tsp. salt

½ tsp. ground chipotle chile pepper
2 cups chopped cooked chicken
1½ cups shredded cheddar cheese (6 oz.)
Refrigerated salsa and/or sliced green onions (optional)

1. Prepare Deep-Dish Pastry Shell. Preheat oven to 400°F. Line pastry with a double thickness of foil, extending foil over side. Bake 20 minutes or until edge of pastry is light brown. Remove foil; bake 10 to 15 minutes more or until bottom is light brown. Cool completely on a wire rack.

2. Preheat oven to 325°F. In a blender combine the next seven ingredients (through ground chipotle pepper). Cover and blend until frothy. Place chicken and cheese in pastry shell; add egg mixture. Place springform pan in a shallow baking pan.

3. Bake 80 to 90 minutes or just until top is lightly browned and filling is set in center (165°F). Cool in pan on a wire rack 40 minutes. Remove side of pan. If desired, serve quiche with salsa and/or green onions. Makes 10 servings.

Deep-Dish Pastry Shell In a food processor combine 2 cups all-purpose flour and 1 tsp. salt. Add 8 Tbsp. cold unsalted butter, cut into small pieces; cover and pulse until mixture resembles coarse crumbs. Combine 1 lightly beaten egg and ¼ cup cold water; add to flour mixture. Cover and pulse just until pastry begins to stick together. Transfer to plastic wrap. Cover; shape into a disk. Chill at least 30 minutes. On a lightly floured surface, roll pastry into a 15-inch circle. Transfer to a 9-inch springform pan; gently press into pan. Trim overhanging pastry to 1 inch and press firmly against edge. Fill any cracks with trimmings. Freeze pastry shell 20 minutes.

PER SERVING *385 cal., 21 g fat (11 g sat. fat), 199 mg chol., 563 mg sodium, 23 g carb., 1 g fiber, 25 g pro.*

HAM AND SWISS WAFFLES WITH MUSTARD SOUR CREAM

CHIPOTLE CHICKEN QUICHE

STUFFED WAFFLES

START TO FINISH 35 minutes

1¾ cups all-purpose flour
1 Tbsp. sugar
2 tsp. baking powder
½ tsp. salt
2 eggs, lightly beaten
1 cup buttermilk or sour milk*
½ cup milk
½ cup vegetable oil
2 Tbsp. chopped fresh basil or sage
1 cup chopped Roma tomatoes
3 oz. white cheddar cheese, shredded
6 slices bacon, crisp-cooked and chopped
  Black pepper
  Pepper jelly, honey butter, and/or sour cream (optional)

1. In a large bowl stir together flour, sugar, baking powder, and salt. In a medium bowl combine eggs, buttermilk, milk, and oil. Add egg mixture all at once to flour mixture. Stir just until moistened. (Batter should be slightly lumpy.)
2. Lightly grease waffle baker and preheat. Reserving a few tablespoons, add batter to waffle baker according to manufacturer's directions. Sprinkle with some of the basil, tomato, cheese, bacon, and pepper. Spoon reserved batter on top to mostly cover toppings. Bake until golden. Repeat with remaining batter. If desired, top with additional basil, tomato, and bacon. Serve with pepper jelly, honey butter, and/or sour cream. Makes 12 servings.

*Tip To make sour milk place 1 Tbsp. lemon juice or vinegar in a liquid measuring cup. Add enough milk to equal 1 cup. Stir; let stand 5 minutes before using.
Make Ahead Layer cooled waffles between sheets of waxed paper. Freeze in an airtight container up to 3 months. To reheat, warm waffles in a toaster.
PER SERVING *229 cal., 15 g fat (4 g sat. fat), 44 mg chol., 307 mg sodium, 17 g carb., 1 g fiber, 7 g pro.*

APPLE FRITTERS

START TO FINISH 35 minutes

  Vegetable oil for deep-fat frying
1⅓ cups all-purpose flour
¼ cup granulated sugar
1 tsp. baking powder
1 tsp. ground cinnamon
½ tsp. salt
½ tsp. lemon zest
2 eggs
⅔ cup milk
1 Tbsp. butter, melted, or vegetable oil
2 medium tart apples, such as Jonathan, Braeburn, or Granny Smith, cored and chopped
  Powdered sugar or Powdered Sugar Icing (recipe, page 62)

1. In a large heavy saucepan or deep-fat fryer heat oil to 365°F. (If using an electric fryer, follow manufacturer's directions.)
2. Meanwhile, in a large bowl whisk together the next six ingredients (through lemon zest). In a small bowl whisk together eggs, milk, and butter. Add egg mixture to flour mixture; stir to combine. Fold in apples.
3. Drop batter by rounded tablespoons, five to six at a time, into hot oil. Cook 4 to 5 minutes or until golden and cooked through, turning once. Remove with a slotted spoon and drain on paper towels. Sprinkle generously with powdered sugar or drizzle with icing. Serve warm. Makes 24 servings.
PER SERVING *84 cal., 4 g fat (1 g sat. fat), 17 mg chol., 82 mg sodium, 10 g carb., 1 g fiber, 2 g pro.*

STUFFED WAFFLES

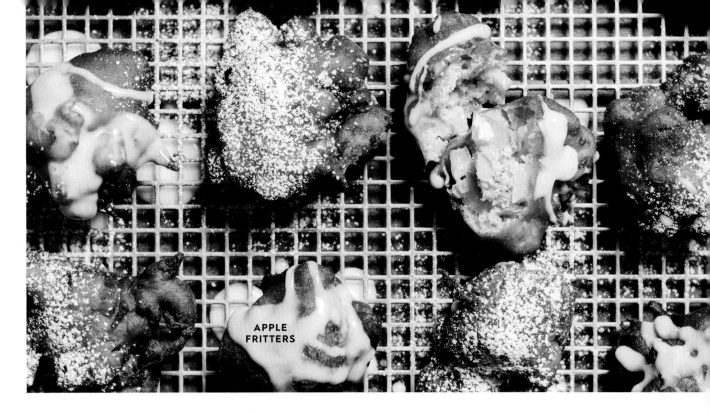

APPLE
FRITTERS

CRANBERRY MUFFINS

PREP 20 minutes
BAKE 15 minutes at 400°F
COOL 10 minutes

1   cup fresh cranberries or
    blueberries
2   Tbsp. sugar
2   cups all-purpose flour
⅓   cup sugar
4   tsp. baking powder
1   tsp. orange zest
½   tsp. salt
1   egg, lightly beaten
¾   cup buttermilk
¼   cup butter, melted
    Coarse sugar

1. Preheat oven to 400°F. Grease twelve
2½-inch muffin cups, line with paper
bake cups, or line with parchment
paper squares. In a medium bowl toss
cranberries with 2 Tbsp. sugar.
2. In a large bowl combine flour, ⅓ cup
sugar, baking powder, orange zest, and
salt; stir well. In a small bowl combine
egg, buttermilk, and butter. Make a
well in center of flour mixture; add egg
mixture and cranberries. Stir just until
moistened. Spoon into prepared muffin
cups. Sprinkle with coarse sugar.
3. Bake 15 minutes or until golden and a
toothpick inserted in center comes out
clean. Cool 10 minutes on a wire rack.
Serve warm. Makes 12 servings.
PER SERVING *163 cal., 5 g fat*
(3 g sat. fat), 29 mg chol., 306 mg
sodium, 27 g carb., 1 g fiber, 3 g pro.

CRANBERRY
MUFFINS

APPLE, CHEDDAR, AND
BACON SCUFFINS

APPLE, CHEDDAR, AND BACON SCUFFINS

PREP 25 minutes
BAKE 20 minutes at 350°F
COOL 25 minutes

    Nonstick cooking spray
1   egg, lightly beaten
1   cup heavy cream or milk
3   cups all-purpose flour
1   Tbsp. sugar
1   Tbsp. baking powder
¼   tsp. salt
½   cup butter
⅔   cup finely chopped tart red apple,
    such as Braeburn
½   cup shredded cheddar cheese
    (2 oz.)
6   slices crisp-cooked bacon,
    crumbled
½   cup apple jelly

1. Preheat oven to 350°F. Coat twelve 2½-inch muffin cups with cooking spray or line with paper bake cups; coat bake cups with cooking spray. Set aside. In a small bowl combine egg and cream.

2. In a large bowl stir together flour, sugar, baking powder, and salt. Using a pastry blender, cut in butter until mixture resembles coarse crumbs. Stir in apple, cheese, and crumbled bacon. Make a well in center of flour mixture. Add egg mixture all at once to flour mixture. Using a fork, stir just until moistened.

3. Spoon half the batter in prepared muffin cups, filling each about half full. Firmly pat into an even layer. Using a spoon or thumb, indent the center of dough in each cup; fill each indentation with 2 tsp. apple jelly. Spoon remaining batter into muffin cups. Gently press layers. If desired, brush lightly with additional cream.

4. Bake 20 to 25 minutes or until tops are golden. Cool in muffin cups on a wire rack 5 minutes. Remove from muffin cups. Cool 20 minutes. Makes 12 servings.

PER SERVING *338 cal., 19 g fat (11 g sat. fat), 67 mg chol., 345 mg sodium, 37 g carb., 1 g fiber, 7 g pro.*

PEANUT BUTTER-STREUSEL MUFFINS

PREP 30 minutes
BAKE 22 minutes at 375°F
COOL 5 minutes

1¼   cups all-purpose flour
¾   cup packed brown sugar
3   Tbsp. butter
2   Tbsp. peanut butter
¼   cup chopped peanuts
½   cup miniature semisweet
     chocolate pieces
¼   cup peanut butter
½   cup milk
1   egg
1   tsp. baking powder
¼   tsp. baking soda
¼   tsp. salt

1. Preheat oven to 375°F. Line twelve 2½-inch muffin cups with paper bake cups; set aside. For streusel topping, in a small bowl stir together ¼ cup flour and ¼ cup brown sugar. Using a pastry blender, cut in 1 Tbsp. butter and 2 Tbsp. peanut butter until mixture resembles coarse crumbs. Stir in peanuts and ¼ cup chocolate pieces. Set aside.

2. In a large bowl combine the remaining 2 Tbsp. butter and ¼ cup peanut butter. Beat with a mixer on medium to high 30 seconds or until combined. Add ½ cup of the remaining flour, the remaining ½ cup brown sugar, half the milk, the egg, baking powder, baking soda, and salt. Beat on low until combined, scraping sides of bowl. Add remaining flour and milk. Beat on low to medium just until combined. Stir in ¼ cup chocolate pieces.

3. Spoon batter into prepared muffin cups, filling each about two-thirds full. Sprinkle with streusel topping. Bake 22 to 25 minutes or until a toothpick inserted near centers comes out clean.

4. Cool in muffin cups on a wire rack 5 minutes. Remove from muffin cups. Serve warm. Makes 12 servings.

PER SERVING *255 cal., 12 g fat (5 g sat. fat), 26 mg chol., 191 mg sodium, 33 g carb., 1 g fiber, 6 g pro.*

CRANBERRY PULL-APART COFFEE CAKE

PREP 10 minutes
BAKE 25 minutes at 350°F

2   12-oz. tubes refrigerated flaky layers biscuits (10 biscuits each), separated and cut into quarters
½   cup packed brown sugar
1   tsp. ground cinnamon
½   tsp. ground ginger
1   cup dried cranberries
1   cup chopped pecans
½   cup butter, melted
2   cups powdered sugar
1   tsp. vanilla
3   to 4 Tbsp. milk

1. Preheat oven to 350°F. Grease a 13×9-inch baking pan. Evenly arrange biscuit quarters in pan. In a small bowl stir together brown sugar, cinnamon, and ginger. Sprinkle over biscuits in pan. Top with cranberries and pecans. Drizzle with butter.

2. Bake 25 to 30 minutes or until golden. Cool slightly in pan on a wire rack.

3. In a small bowl stir together powdered sugar, vanilla, and enough milk to reach drizzling consistency. Drizzle over coffee cake. Serve warm. Makes 12 servings.

PER SERVING *420 cal., 18 g fat (6 g sat. fat), 21 mg chol., 553 mg sodium, 64 g carb., 2 g fiber, 5 g pro.*
Variation Substitute chopped dried apricots, cherries, dates, or raisins for the cranberries; swap walnuts, macadamia nuts, hazelnuts, or almonds for the pecans. Or sprinkle flaked coconut and mini chocolate chips.

PEANUT BUTTER-STREUSEL MUFFINS

CRANBERRY PULL-APART COFFEE CAKE

JUMBO APPLE CINNAMON ROLLS

PREP 45 minutes
RISE 1 hour 15 minutes
REST 10 minutes
BAKE 25 minutes at 375°F

2¾ to 3½ cups all-purpose flour
1   pkg. active dry yeast
⅔   cup mashed, cooked potato*
½   cup milk
3   Tbsp. butter, cut up
3   Tbsp. granulated sugar
½   tsp. salt
2   eggs
1   cup finely chopped peeled apples
2   tsp. ground cinnamon or apple
     pie spice
½   cup packed brown sugar
3   Tbsp. butter, softened
1   recipe Cream Cheese Icing
     (optional)

1. In a large bowl combine 1 cup flour and yeast. In a small saucepan heat potato, milk, butter, granulated sugar, and salt, stirring frequently, just until warm (120°F to 130°F) and butter is almost melted; add to flour mixture. Add eggs. Beat with a mixer on low 30 seconds, scraping bowl constantly. Beat on high 3 minutes. Stir in as much remaining flour as you can.

2. Turn dough out onto a lightly floured surface. Knead in enough remaining flour to make a moderately soft dough that is smooth and elastic (3 to 5 minutes). Shape dough into a ball. Place in a lightly greased bowl; turn to grease surface of dough. Cover and let rise in a warm place until double in size (45 to 60 minutes).

3. Punch dough down. Turn out onto a lightly floured surface. Cover and let rest 10 minutes. Meanwhile, grease a 10- to 12-inch cast-iron skillet. For filling, in a small bowl stir together apples, cinnamon, and brown sugar.

4. Roll dough into a 15×10-inch rectangle. Spread with softened butter and sprinkle with filling, leaving 1 inch unfilled along one long side. Tightly roll up, starting from filled long side, seal seams with fingertips. Press ends of roll toward center, shaping a 12-inch roll. Cut into 6 slices.

5. Place slices, cut sides on brown sugar mixture in skillet. Cover and let rise in a warm place until nearly double in size (30 minutes).

6. Preheat oven to 375°F. Bake 25 minutes or until golden. If needed to prevent overbrowning, cover loosely with foil the last 5 to 10 minutes. Serve warm rolls directly from skillet. If desired, frost with Cream Cheese Icing. Or invert rolls onto a platter (spoon any caramel remaining in pan onto rolls). Makes 6 servings.

*Tip Prick an 8- to 10-oz. unpeeled potato all over with a fork. Microwave 5 to 7 minutes or until tender. Halve potato and scoop pulp out of skin into a small bowl; discard skin. Mash potato pulp. Measure ⅔ cup mashed potato.

Make Ahead Prepare rolls as directed through Step 4, except do not let rise after shaping. Cover loosely with oiled waxed paper, then with plastic wrap. Chill 2 to 24 hours. Before baking, let chilled rolls stand, covered, at room temperature 30 minutes. Uncover and bake as directed.

PER SERVING *398 cal., 14 g fat (8 g sat. fat), 94 mg chol., 321 mg sodium, 58 g carb., 3 g fiber, 10 g pro.*

Cream Cheese Icing In a medium bowl beat 3-oz. softened cream cheese, 2 Tbsp. softened butter, and 1 tsp. vanilla with a mixer on medium until combined. Gradually beat in 2½ cups powdered sugar until smooth. Beat in enough milk, 1 tsp. at a time, to reach spreading consistency.

JUMBO APPLE CINNAMON ROLLS

ESPRESSO MONKEY ROLLS

PREP 25 minutes
BAKE 18 minutes at 350°F
COOL 3 minutes

1	cup packed brown sugar
2	tsp. ground cinnamon
1	tsp. instant espresso coffee powder
½	cup butter, melted
1	tsp. vanilla
3	11-oz. pkg. refrigerated breadsticks (12 each)
1	recipe Espresso Icing

1. Preheat oven to 350°F. Generously grease eighteen 2½-inch muffin cups.
2. In a bowl stir together brown sugar, cinnamon, and espresso powder. In another bowl stir together butter and 1 tsp. vanilla.
3. Unroll breadstick dough and separate into 36 strips. Roll each strip into a spiral. Dip each dough spiral into butter mixture; then roll in brown sugar mixture to coat. Arrange two spirals in each cup. Sprinkle any remaining brown sugar mixture on tops. Drizzle any remaining butter on tops.
4. Place an extra-large baking sheet on rack below muffin cups. Bake 18 minutes or until puffed and brown. (If needed, cover rolls loosely with foil to prevent overbrowning.) Cool on a wire rack 3 minutes. Remove rolls from cups. Drizzle any melted sugar mixture remaining in muffin cups over rolls. Drizzle rolls with Espresso Icing; serve warm. Makes 18 servings.

Espresso Icing Stir together 2 Tbsp. milk, 1 Tbsp. instant espresso powder, and 1 tsp. vanilla until espresso powder is dissolved. Stir in 1½ cups powdered sugar. If needed, stir in additional milk, 1 tsp. at a time, to reach drizzling consistency.
Make Ahead Prepare and bake as directed. Cool completely. Wrap tightly in foil. Store at room temperature up to 2 days. To reheat, preheat oven to 350°F. Heat rolls in foil 5 to 10 minutes or until warm.
PER SERVING *265 cal., 7 g fat (3 g sat. fat), 14 mg chol., 425 mg sodium, 49 g carb., 1 g fiber, 4 g pro.*

PUMPKIN CRUMB CAKE

COCONUT-OAT GRANOLA

PUMPKIN CRUMB CAKE

PREP 25 minutes
BAKE 40 minutes at 350°F

1½   cups packed brown sugar
⅔   cup all-purpose flour
⅔   cup regular rolled oats
6   Tbsp. butter
½   cup chopped pecans
2½   cups all-purpose flour
2   tsp. baking soda
2   tsp. ground cinnamon
½   tsp. salt
½   tsp. ground nutmeg
½   tsp. ground cloves
1   cup granulated sugar
¾   cup shortening
2   eggs
1   15-oz. can pumpkin

1. Preheat oven to 350°F. Grease a 13×9-inch baking pan. For topping, in a bowl combine ½ cup brown sugar, ⅔ cup flour, and oats. Using a pastry blender, cut in butter until pieces are pea size. Stir in pecans.
2. In a large bowl combine butter, pecans, 2½ cups flour, baking soda, cinnamon, salt, nutmeg, and cloves.
3. In an extra-large bowl beat sugar, shortening, eggs, and remaining 1 cup brown sugar with a mixer on medium 2 minutes. Alternately add flour mixture and pumpkin, beating on low after each addition just until combined.
4. Spread batter in prepared pan; sprinkle with topping. Bake 40 minutes or until a toothpick inserted in center comes out clean and topping is golden. Cool in pan on a wire rack. Makes 16 servings.
PER SERVING *396 cal., 18 g fat (6 g sat. fat), 35 mg chol., 281 mg sodium, 57 g carb., 2 g fiber, 4 g pro.*

COCONUT-OAT GRANOLA

PREP 15 minutes
BAKE 35 minutes at 325°F

⅓   cup unsweetened applesauce
3   Tbsp. flaxseed meal
2   Tbsp. chia seeds
2   Tbsp. pure maple syrup
1   Tbsp. coconut oil
2   tsp. orange zest
1   tsp. vanilla
½   tsp. salt
½   tsp. ground cinnamon
3   cups regular rolled oats
½   cup pepitas
½   cup unsweetened flaked coconut, toasted (tip, page 96)
      Fat-free yogurt or fat-free milk (optional)
      Maple syrup or honey (optional)

1. Preheat oven to 325°F. Line a 15×10-inch baking pan with foil or parchment paper. In a bowl stir together the first nine ingredients (through cinnamon). Add oats and pepitas; stir to coat. Spread oat mixture in prepared pan; pat lightly.
2. Bake 35 minutes or until golden, stirring and spreading evenly halfway through. While warm, stir in coconut. Cool completely. If desired, serve with yogurt or milk and/or drizzle with maple syrup or honey. Makes 8 servings.
PER SERVING *280 cal., 15 g fat (5 g sat. fat), 0 mg chol., 184 mg sodium, 30 g carb., 7 g fiber, 10 g pro.*

PUMPKIN WAFFLES WITH MAPLE-WALNUT CREAM

PREP 15 minutes
BAKE according to manufacturer's directions

- 4 cups all-purpose flour
- ¼ cup packed brown sugar
- 2 Tbsp. baking powder
- 1 tsp. salt
- 1 tsp. ground cinnamon
- ½ tsp. ground ginger
- ½ tsp. ground nutmeg
- 4 eggs, lightly beaten
- 3 cups milk
- 1 15-oz. can pumpkin
- ¼ cup butter, melted
- 1 recipe Maple-Walnut Cream

1. Lightly grease and preheat waffle baker. Preheat oven to 300°F.

2. In a large bowl stir together the first seven ingredients (through nutmeg). Make a well in center of flour mixture.

3. In another large bowl combine eggs, milk, pumpkin, and butter. Add pumpkin mixture all at once to flour mixture. Stir just until moistened (batter should be slightly lumpy).

4. Add batter to waffle baker according to manufacturer's directions. Close lid quickly; do not open until done. Bake according to manufacturer's directions. When done, use a fork to lift waffle off grid. Place on a baking sheet in oven to keep warm. Repeat with remaining batter. Serve warm with Maple-Walnut Cream. Makes 12 servings.

Maple-Walnut Cream In a medium saucepan melt 1 Tbsp. butter over medium heat. Add ¾ cup walnuts; cook and stir 1 to 2 minutes or until walnuts are toasted. Stir in 1½ cups maple syrup and ½ cup heavy cream; heat through.

PER SERVING 466 cal., 17 g fat (7 g sat. fat), 102 mg chol., 408 mg sodium, 71 g carb., 3 g fiber, 10 g pro.

PUMPKIN WAFFLES WITH MAPLE-WALNUT CREAM

CITRUS MOCK
MIMOSAS

SPICED
PEAR TEA

CITRUS MOCK MIMOSAS

PREP 10 minutes
CHILL 2 hours

1½ cups fresh orange juice
1 cup fresh grapefruit juice
½ cup fresh lime juice
2 to 4 Tbsp. honey
2 12-oz. bottles sparkling water, chilled
   Pineapple wedges (optional)

1. In a 4-cup glass measure combine orange juice, grapefruit juice, lime juice, and honey. Stir until honey is dissolved. Cover and chill at least 2 hours or up to 24 hours.
2. To serve, pour juice mixture into four champagne glasses. Add sparkling water and stir lightly to mix. If desired, serve with pineapple wedges. Makes 8 servings.
PER SERVING *53 cal., 0 g fat, 0 mg chol., 19 mg sodium, 13 g carb., 0 g fiber, 1 g pro.*

SPICED PEAR TEA

PREP 10 minutes
COOK 10 minutes
STAND 5 minutes

1 orange
3 cups water
2 11.3- to 12-oz. can pear nectar
1 Tbsp. honey (optional)
4 inches stick cinnamon
1 tsp. whole cloves
6 tea bags
   Thinly sliced apple (optional)

1. Using a vegetable peeler, remove three wide strips of peel from the orange; set peel aside. Juice the orange into a large saucepan.
2. Add water, pear nectar, and honey (if using) to orange juice in saucepan. For spice bag, place stick cinnamon, cloves, and orange peel strips in center of 6-inch square, double-thick 100-percent-cotton cheesecloth. Bring corners together and tie with clean kitchen string. Add spice bag to pear nectar mixture.
3. Bring mixture to boiling; reduce heat. Cover and simmer 10 minutes. Remove from heat. Add tea bags; cover and let stand 5 minutes. Remove and discard tea bags and spice bag. If desired, serve with apple slices. Makes 8 servings.
PER SERVING *57 cal., 0 g fat, 0 mg chol., 6 mg sodium, 15 g carb., 1 g fiber, 0 g pro.*

VANILLA CAFÉ LATTE

START TO FINISH 5 minutes

¼ cup hot espresso or strong coffee
2 tsp. vanilla-flavor syrup or 1 tsp. sugar and ¼ tsp. vanilla
2 to 3 Tbsp. steamed milk
2 Tbsp. frothed milk*
   Ground cinnamon or grated chocolate

1. Pour espresso or coffee into a 6-oz. cup. Stir in vanilla syrup. Add steamed milk and top with frothed milk. Sprinkle with cinnamon. Makes 1 serving.
*Tip To froth milk, place hot (not boiling) milk in a blender. Cover and blend until froth forms. Or place hot milk in a deep bowl and carefully use an immersion blender until frothy.
PER SERVING *55 cal., 1 g fat (0 g sat. fat), 5 mg chol., 26 mg sodium, 9 g carb., 0 g fiber, 2 g pro.*

VANILLA
CAFÉ LATTE

GINGERBREAD-
SOUR CREAM
MUFFINS, PAGE 75

Sweet and Savory Breads

Indulge in the joys of baking this season, and enchant family
and guests with extraordinary breads, rolls, muffins, scones
and popovers.

CARROT CAKE
BREAD, PAGE 71

PARMESAN
DINNER ROLLS

PARMESAN DINNER ROLLS

PREP 25 minutes
RISE 30 minutes
BAKE 12 minutes at 400°F

1   16-oz. pkg. hot roll mix
¼   cup finely shredded Parmesan cheese (1 oz.)
2   Tbsp. sugar
2   Tbsp. snipped fresh basil or 1 tsp. dried basil, crushed
1   Tbsp. milk
2   Tbsp. finely shredded Parmesan cheese

1. Grease twenty-four 1¾-inch muffin cups; set aside. In a large bowl prepare hot roll mix according to package directions (stirring ¼ cup cheese, the sugar, and basil into flour mixture), through the resting step.
2. Using a knife, divide dough in half. Divide each half into 12 portions (24 portions total). Gently pull each portion into a ball, tucking edges beneath. Arrange balls, smooth sides up, in prepared muffin cups. Cover and let rise in a warm place until nearly double in size (about 30 minutes).
3. Preheat oven to 400°F. Using a pastry brush, brush tops of rolls with milk; sprinkle with 2 Tbsp. cheese. Bake 12 to 15 minutes or until tops are golden. Serve warm. Makes 24 servings.
Make Ahead Prepare and bake rolls as directed; cool completely. Wrap rolls in foil and freeze up to 2 days. To serve, preheat oven to 350°F. Reheat wrapped frozen rolls 20 minutes or until heated through.
PER SERVING *70 cal., 1 g fat (0 g sat. fat), 1 mg chol., 137 mg sodium, 13 g carb., 0 g fiber, 3 g pro.*

CRACKED BLACK PEPPER AND ROSEMARY FOCACCIA

PREP 25 minutes
RISE 1 hour
REST 20 minutes
BAKE 25 minutes at 375°F

2¾ cups all-purpose flour
1   pkg. active dry yeast
½   tsp. salt
1   cup warm water (120°F to 130°F)
2   Tbsp. olive oil

CRACKED BLACK PEPPER AND ROSEMARY FOCACCIA

1   cup whole wheat flour
2   cloves garlic, thinly sliced
½   cup pitted Kalamata or ripe olives, halved or sliced (optional)
1   tsp. snipped fresh rosemary or ½ tsp. dried rosemary, crushed
½   tsp. kosher salt
½   tsp. cracked black pepper
½   cup finely shredded Parmesan cheese (2 oz.)

1. In a large bowl combine all-purpose flour, yeast, and salt; add warm water and olive oil. Beat with a mixer on low 30 seconds. Beat on high 3 minutes. Stir in whole wheat flour. Turn dough out onto a lightly floured surface. Knead in an additional ¼ to ½ cup whole wheat flour to make a moderately stiff dough that is smooth and elastic (3 to 4 minutes total). Cover and let rest 10 minutes.

2. Place dough in a lightly oiled medium bowl turning once to oil surface. Cover and let rise in a warm place 30 minutes. Punch dough down. Let rest 10 minutes. Place dough on a large greased or parchment-lined baking sheet. Press dough into a 13×9-inch rectangle.
3. Brush additional olive oil on dough. Sprinkle with garlic, olives (if using), rosemary, salt, cracked black pepper, and cheese. Place baking sheet in a warm place; cover and let rise 30 minutes.
4. Preheat oven to 375°F. Bake 25 minutes or until golden brown. Cool slightly. Cut into squares. Makes 16 servings.
PER SERVING *109 cal., 4 g fat (1 g sat. fat), 2 mg chol., 236 mg sodium, 15 g carb., 2 g fiber, 3 g pro.*

CHOCOLATE
PANETTONE
BUNS

Powdered Sugar Icing
In a small bowl stir together 1 cup powdered sugar, 1 Tbsp. milk, and ½ tsp. vanilla. Stir in additional milk, 1 tsp. at a time, to reach drizzling consistency.

PER SERVING *348 cal., 13 g fat (7 g sat. fat), 68 mg chol., 191 mg sodium, 53 g carb., 3 g fiber, 7 g pro.*

CAST-IRON CINNAMON ROLLS

PREP 20 minutes
RISE 45 minutes
BAKE 40 minutes at 350°F

½   cup packed brown sugar
¼   cup granulated sugar
1   Tbsp. ground cinnamon
2   16-oz. loaves frozen white bread dough, thawed
⅓   cup butter, melted
½   cup chopped pecans or walnuts (optional)
1   cup canned or homemade cream cheese frosting

1. Grease and flour a 10- or 12-inch cast-iron skillet; set aside. In a small bowl combine brown sugar, granulated sugar, and cinnamon.
2. On a lightly floured surface, roll each loaf of dough into a 15×7 inch rectangle, pausing occasionally to let dough relax if necessary. Generously brush each rectangle with melted butter; sprinkle with sugar mixture (and nuts if using). Pat the sugar firmly on dough. Cut each rectangle lengthwise into seven 1-inch strips. Roll one strip into a loose spiral to shape center of cinnamon roll; gently place in center of prepared skillet. Gently wrap remaining dough strips adjacent to center roll in a loose spiral. Cover and let rise in a warm place until nearly double in size (45 to 60 minutes)
3. Meanwhile, preheat oven to 350°F. Bake rolls 40 to 45 minutes or until golden brown (195°F to 200°F). Spread with frosting while warm. Makes 16 servings.

PER SERVING *282 cal., 9 g fat (3 g sat. fat), 10 mg chol., 332 mg sodium, 47 g carb., 1 g fiber, 3 g pro.*

CHOCOLATE PANETTONE BUNS

PREP 30 minutes
RISE 1 hour 45 minutes
BAKE 12 minutes at 375°F

3¼   cups all-purpose flour
¼   cup unsweetened cocoa powder
1   pkg. active dry yeast
½   cup butter
½   cup milk
2   oz. dark or bittersweet chocolate, finely chopped (⅓ cup)
¼   cup sugar
½   tsp. salt
3   eggs
1   Tbsp. orange juice or milk
1   tsp. vanilla
⅓   cup diced candied orange peel
⅓   cup snipped dried cherries or cranberries
⅓   cup slivered almonds, toasted and chopped (tip, page 22)
1   recipe Powdered Sugar Icing

1. In a large bowl stir together 2¼ cups of the flour, cocoa powder, and yeast. In a medium saucepan heat and stir butter, milk, chocolate, sugar, and salt over medium-low just until warm (120°F to 130°F) and butter is almost melted.
2. Add milk mixture to flour mixture. Add eggs, orange juice, and vanilla. Beat with a mixer on medium 30 seconds, scraping sides of bowl constantly. Beat on high 3 minutes.
3. Stir in remaining flour, candied orange peel, dried cherries, and almonds. Cover dough and let rise in a warm place until double in size (about 1 hour).
4. Punch dough down and turn out onto a lightly floured surface. Cover and let rest 10 minutes. Meanwhile, lightly grease a large baking sheet.
5. Divide dough into 12 pieces. Gently shape each piece into a ball, tucking under edges. Place balls 2 to 3 inches apart on prepared baking sheet. Cover loosely with oiled plastic wrap and let rise in a warm place until nearly double in size (about 45 minutes).
6. Preheat oven to 375°F. Uncover buns. Bake 12 to 15 minutes or until bottoms are brown and buns sound hollow when lightly tapped. Transfer to a wire rack; cool. Drizzle with Powdered Sugar Icing. Makes 12 servings.

CAST-IRON
CINNAMON ROLLS

MAPLE-PEAR
PULL-APART
BREAD

MAPLE-PEAR PULL-APART BREAD

PREP 25 minutes
RISE 1 hour 25 minutes
BAKE 45 minutes at 350°F
COOL 10 minutes
STAND 5 minutes

¾ cup milk
1 pkg. active dry yeast
1 egg, lightly beaten
¼ cup butter, melted
2 Tbsp. maple syrup
½ tsp. salt
3 cups all-purpose flour
¼ cup butter, melted
1½ cups peeled, cored, finely chopped pears
¾ cup packed brown sugar
1 tsp. ground cardamom
¾ cup powdered sugar
2 to 3 Tbsp. maple syrup

1. In a small saucepan heat milk until warm (105°F to 115°F). In a large bowl combine warm milk and yeast; stir until yeast is dissolved. Let stand 5 minutes.
2. Add egg, ¼ cup of the melted butter, 2 Tbsp. maple syrup, and salt to yeast mixture. Beat with a mixer on medium until combined. Add half the flour; beat on low 30 seconds, scraping bowl as needed. Beat 1 minute on medium. Stir in remaining flour. Shape dough into a ball (dough will not be smooth). Place in a greased bowl; turn once to grease surface. Cover; let rise in a warm place until nearly double in size (45 to 60 minutes).
3. Grease a 9×5-inch loaf pan. Turn dough out onto a lightly floured surface. Roll dough into a 20×12-inch rectangle. Brush dough with remaining ¼ cup melted butter.
4. Sprinkle dough with pears, brown sugar, and cardamom. Cut rectangle in half lengthwise for two 20×6-inch strips. Cut each strip crosswise into five 6×4-inch strips. Make two stacks of five strips each. Cut each stack into three 4×2-inch sections. Stagger sections in pan, cut sides up. Cover; let rise in a warm place until nearly double in size (40 to 45 minutes).
5. Preheat oven to 350°F. Bake 45 minutes or until golden brown and an instant-read thermometer inserted near center registers 200°F. Cool in pan 10 minutes. Transfer to a serving plate.

CHEDDAR-GREEN ONION POPOVERS

Stir together powdered sugar and 2 to 3 Tbsp. maple syrup to make drizzling consistency. Drizzle over loaf. Makes 10 servings.
Make Ahead Prepare as directed through Step 2, except do not let dough rise. Cover bowl and refrigerate up to 24 hours. Let dough stand at room temperature 30 minutes before continuing with Step 3.
PER SERVING 370 cal., 11 g fat (6 g sat. fat), 44 mg chol., 212 mg sodium, 64 g carb., 2 g fiber, 6 g pro.

CHEDDAR-GREEN ONION POPOVERS

PREP 10 minutes
BAKE 15 minutes at 450°F/10 minutes at 350°F

Nonstick cooking spray
1 cup all-purpose flour
½ tsp. salt
2 eggs
1 cup milk
1 cup shredded sharp cheddar cheese
3 green onions, trimmed and chopped

1. Preheat oven to 450°F. Coat eight cups of a popover or standard muffin pan with cooking spray. (Fill any empty cups with ½ inch water to prevent pan from burning.)
2. In a medium bowl whisk together flour and salt. In another bowl whisk together eggs and milk; add to flour mixture; stir just until blended. Fold in cheese and green onions.
3. Fill prepared cups about three-fourths full. Bake 15 minutes. Reduce oven temperature to 350°F. Bake 10 to 15 minutes, until browned and puffed. Keep oven closed until end of baking time to prevent popovers from deflating.
4. Remove popovers from oven and immediately remove from pan. Pierce sides once with a knife to release steam. Serve warm. Makes 8 servings.
PER SERVING 150 cal., 7 g fat (0 g sat. fat), 71 mg chol., 263 mg sodium, 14 g carb., 1 g fiber, 8 g pro.

CURRANT-ORANGE IRISH SODA BREAD

PREP 20 minutes
BAKE 30 minutes at 375°F

2	cups all-purpose flour
1	to 2 Tbsp. sugar
1	tsp. baking powder
½	tsp. baking soda
½	tsp. salt
1	Tbsp. orange zest
3	Tbsp. butter
⅓	cup currants
1	egg, lightly beaten
¾	cup buttermilk

1. Preheat oven to 375°F. Grease a baking sheet. In a large bowl stir together flour, sugar, baking powder, baking soda, salt, and orange zest. Cut in butter until mixture resembles coarse crumbs. Stir in currants. Make a well in center of flour mixture.
2. In a small bowl stir together egg and buttermilk. Add all at once to flour mixture. Stir just until moistened.
3. On a lightly floured surface gently knead dough to form a dough (four or five times) that's smooth and elastic. Shape into a 7-inch round loaf.
4. Transfer dough to prepared baking sheet. With a sharp knife, score top to form an X. Bake 30 to 35 minutes or until golden. Serve warm. Makes 12 servings.
PER SERVING *129 cal., 4 g fat (2 g sat. fat), 26 mg chol., 192 mg sodium, 21 g carb., 1 g fiber, 3 g pro.*

PIZZA CHEESE POCKETS

PREP 25 minutes
BAKE 30 minutes at 375°F

	Nonstick cooking spray
1	13.8-oz. pkg. refrigerated pizza dough
½	cup miniature sliced pepperoni or chopped pepperoni
6	oz. mozzarella cheese, cut into 24 cubes
1	Tbsp. olive oil
¼	cup finely shredded Parmesan cheese (1 oz.)
	Pizza sauce, warmed

1. Preheat oven to 375°F. Coat an 8-inch square baking dish with cooking spray.
2. On a lightly floured surface, unroll pizza dough and press into a 12×8-inch rectangle. Using a pizza cutter or sharp knife, cut dough into twenty-four 2-inch squares. Top with pepperoni and mozzarella cheese. Bring dough up around pepperoni and mozzarella cheese to enclose; pinch edges together to seal. Place, seam sides down, in prepared dish.
3. Drizzle dough with oil; sprinkle with Parmesan cheese. Bake 30 to 35 minutes or until golden. Serve warm with pizza sauce. Makes 12 servings.
Make Ahead Prepare as directed through Step 2. Cover with plastic wrap; chill 2 to 8 hours. Let stand at room temperature 30 minutes. Continue as directed in Step 3.
PER SERVING *180 cal., 8 g fat (4 g sat. fat), 18 mg chol., 565 mg sodium, 19 g carb., 1 g fiber, 8 g pro.*

CURRANT-ORANGE IRISH SODA BREAD

PIZZA CHEESE POCKETS

TUSCAN
POLENTA
BREAD

**BAKLAVA
MONKEY BREAD**

TUSCAN POLENTA BREAD

PREP 25 minutes
BAKE 30 minutes at 375°F
STAND 5 minutes

1½ cups cornmeal
½ cup all-purpose flour
2 Tbsp. sugar
1 tsp. baking soda
¼ tsp. salt
2 Tbsp. olive oil
2 eggs, lightly beaten
1¾ cups half-and-half
9 slices bacon or ¾ cup chopped pancetta, crisp-cooked
1 8-oz. jar oil-packed dried tomatoes, drained and snipped
1 Tbsp. chopped shallot
1 Tbsp. chopped fresh rosemary
  Butter, softened (optional)

1. Preheat oven to 375°F. In a medium bowl stir together the first five ingredients (through salt). Add 1 Tbsp. oil to a 10-inch cast-iron skillet. Heat in oven 5 minutes. Remove skillet; carefully swirl oil to coat bottom and sides.

2. Meanwhile, in a large bowl combine eggs, half-and-half, and remaining 1 Tbsp. oil. Crumble bacon. Stir bacon, tomatoes, shallot, and rosemary into egg mixture. Add cornmeal mixture all at once to egg mixture. Stir just until moistened.

3. Pour batter into hot skillet. Bake 30 to 35 minutes or until a toothpick inserted near center comes out clean. Serve warm and, if desired, with butter. Makes 8 servings.

PER SERVING *367 cal., 18 g fat (6 g sat. fat), 82 mg chol., 553 mg sodium, 46 g carb., 2 g fiber, 11 g pro.*

BAKLAVA MONKEY BREAD

PREP 15 minutes
BAKE 40 minutes at 350°F
STAND 5 minutes

⅔ cup packed brown sugar
⅓ cup honey
⅓ cup heavy cream
3 Tbsp. butter
1 tsp. lemon zest
½ cup walnuts, finely chopped
½ cup pistachio nuts, finely chopped
⅓ cup granulated sugar
1 tsp. ground cinnamon
3 7.5-oz. cans refrigerated biscuits (30 total), halved crosswise

1. Preheat oven to 350°F. For syrup, in a medium saucepan combine brown sugar, honey, cream, butter, and lemon zest. Bring to boiling; reduce heat. Simmer, uncovered, 5 minutes or until reduced to 1 cup. Cool slightly.

2. Meanwhile, in a small bowl combine walnuts, pistachios, granulated sugar, and cinnamon. Generously grease a 10-inch cast-iron skillet. Spoon half the nut mixture into prepared skillet. Top with half the dough pieces and drizzle with half the syrup. Repeat layers.

3. Bake 40 minutes or until golden. Let stand 5 minutes; invert onto a platter. Spoon any topping and nuts remaining in pan over bread. Serve warm. Makes 12 servings.

PER SERVING *424 cal., 18 g fat (8 g sat. fat), 15 mg chol., 705 mg sodium, 61 g carb., 3 g fiber, 7 g pro.*

CARROT CAKE
BREAD

CARROT CAKE BREAD

PREP 25 minutes
BAKE 55 minutes at 350°F
COOL 1 hour 10 minutes

1½ cups all-purpose flour
1   tsp. baking powder
½   tsp. salt
½   tsp. ground cinnamon or ¼ tsp. ground ginger
¼   tsp. baking soda
2   eggs, lightly beaten
1½   cups lightly packed, finely shredded carrots
¾   cup vegetable oil
½   cup granulated sugar
½   cup packed brown sugar
1   tsp. vanilla
½   cup chopped candied or glazed pecans or toasted pecans
1   recipe Cream Cheese Drizzle

1. Preheat oven to 350°F. Grease bottom and ½ inch up sides of an 8×4-inch cast-iron loaf pan. In a large bowl stir together the first five ingredients (through baking soda). Make a well in center of flour mixture.
2. In a medium bowl combine eggs, carrots, oil, sugars, and vanilla). Add carrot mixture all at once to flour mixture. Stir just until moistened (batter should be lumpy). Fold in pecans. Spread batter into prepared pan.
3. Bake 55 to 60 minutes or until a toothpick inserted near center comes out clean. Cool in pan on a wire rack 10 minutes. Remove from pan; cool completely on wire rack. Wrap and store overnight before slicing. Before serving, top with cream cheese drizzle and, if desired, additional candied pecans.
Cream Cheese Drizzle In a small bowl stir together 1 oz. cream cheese and 1 Tbsp. softened butter until smooth. Stir in ½ cup powdered sugar and enough milk (about 1 Tbsp.) to make drizzling consistency. Makes 12 servings.
PER SERVING *322 cal., 18 g fat (3 g sat. fat), 36 mg chol., 207 mg sodium, 38 g carb., 1 g fiber, 3 g pro.*

TOASTY WHOLE GRAIN ORANGE MUFFINS

TOASTY WHOLE GRAIN ORANGE MUFFINS

PREP 25 minutes
BAKE 25 minutes at 400°F
COOL 5 minutes

1   cup regular rolled oats
½   cup cooked quinoa, cooled
⅓   cup finely chopped walnuts
1   Tbsp. olive oil
1   cup all-purpose flour
½   cup whole wheat flour
¼   cup sugar
1½   tsp. baking powder
½   tsp. baking soda
½   tsp. salt
½   cup buttermilk
2   eggs
½   cup sour cream
3   Tbsp. butter, melted
1   orange (2 tsp. zest; 3 Tbsp. juice)
     Orange marmalade (optional)

1. Preheat oven to 400°F. Place oats, cooled quinoa, and walnuts in a greased 15×10-inch baking pan; toss to combine. Add oil; toss to coat. Spread in an even layer. Bake 10 to 12 minutes or until toasted, stirring once. Remove; cool in pan on a wire rack.
2. Grease twelve 2½-inch muffin cups; set aside. In a large bowl stir together all but ¼ cup of the oats mixture, the flours, sugar, baking powder, baking soda, and salt. Make a well in center of flour mixture.
3. In a 2-cup measure whisk together buttermilk, eggs, sour cream, butter, and orange zest and juice. Add all at once to flour mixture. Gently stir just until moistened (batter should be lumpy).
4. Spoon batter into prepared muffin cups, filling each three-fourths full. Sprinkle with remaining oats mixture. Bake 15 minutes or until golden. Cool in cups on a wire rack 5 minutes. Serve warm and, if desired, with orange marmalade. Makes 12 servings.
PER SERVING *238 cal., 10 g fat (4 g sat. fat), 43 mg chol., 267 mg sodium, 31 g carb., 3 g fiber, 7 g pro.*

BERRY-CHERRY MUFFINS

PREP 20 minutes
BAKE 15 minutes at 400°F
COOL 5 minutes

2   cups all-purpose flour
¼   cup granulated sugar
1½   tsp. baking powder
½   tsp. baking soda
½   tsp. salt
⅔   cup buttermilk
½   cup sour cream
2   eggs
5   Tbsp. butter, melted
1   cup fresh blueberries and/or
     raspberries
½   cup dried tart red cherries and/or
     cranberries
     Turbinado sugar (optional)

1. Preheat oven to 400°F. Grease twelve
2½-inch muffin cups; set aside. In a large
bowl stir together flour, granulated
sugar, baking powder, baking soda,
and salt. Make a well in the center of
flour mixture.
2. In a 2-cup measure whisk together
buttermilk, sour cream, eggs, and
3 Tbsp. of the melted butter. Add all at
once to flour mixture. Gently stir just until
moistened (batter will be lumpy). Gently
fold in berries and dried fruit.
3. Spoon batter into prepared muffin
cups, filling each three-fourths full.
Bake 15 minutes or until golden
brown. Remove from oven. Brush with
remaining melted butter and, if desired,
sprinkle with turbinado sugar. Cool in
cups on a wire rack 5 minutes. Makes
12 servings.
PER SERVING *191 cal., 8 g fat
(4 g sat. fat), 48 mg chol., 286 mg
sodium, 28 g carb., 1 g fiber, 4 g pro.*

BERRY-CHERRY
MUFFINS

GINGERBREAD-SOUR
CREAM MUFFINS

GINGERBREAD-SOUR CREAM MUFFINS

PREP 20 minutes
BAKE 18 minutes
COOL 5 minutes

2 cups unbleached all-purpose flour or all-purpose flour
1 Tbsp. finely chopped fresh ginger or 1 tsp. ground ginger
2 tsp. baking powder
¾ tsp. ground allspice or cinnamon
¼ tsp. baking soda
¼ tsp. salt
¼ cup cold butter
1 egg, lightly beaten
1 8-oz. carton sour cream
⅓ cup milk
¼ cup packed brown sugar
¼ cup mild-flavor molasses
2 Tbsp. granulated sugar
2 Tbsp. finely snipped crystallized ginger

1. Preheat oven to 400°F. Grease bottoms of twelve 2½-inch muffin cups.
2. In a medium bowl stir together flour, ginger, baking powder, allspice, baking soda, and salt. Using a pastry blender, cut in butter until mixture resembles coarse crumbs. Make a well in center of flour mixture.
3. In another medium bowl stir together egg, sour cream, milk, brown sugar, and molasses. Add egg mixture all at once to flour mixture. Stir just until moistened (batter should be lumpy). Spoon batter into prepared cups, filling each nearly full.
4. In a small bowl combine granulated sugar and crystallized ginger. Sprinkle over muffin batter.
5. Bake 18 to 20 minutes or until golden brown and a toothpick inserted near centers comes out clean. Cool in cups on wire rack 5 minutes. Remove from pan; serve warm. Makes 12 servings.
PER SERVING *211 cal., 9 g fat (5 g sat. fat), 37 mg chol., 168 mg sodium, 30 g carb., 1 g fiber, 4 g pro.*

APPLE-CARROT CAKE MUFFINS

APPLE-CARROT CAKE MUFFINS

PREP 25 minutes
BAKE 20 minutes at 350°F
COOL 10 minutes

2 cups all-purpose flour
1¼ cups sugar
2 tsp. baking soda
1 to 1½ tsp. apple pie spice
½ tsp. salt
2 cups finely shredded carrots
1 cup shredded, peeled apple
½ cup raisins
3 eggs, lightly beaten
⅔ cup vegetable oil
⅓ cup milk
1 tsp. vanilla
1 recipe Coconut Streusel (optional)

1. Preheat oven to 350°F. Grease twenty-four 2½-inch muffin cups or line with paper bake cups.
2. In a large bowl combine the first five ingredients (through salt). Make a well in center of flour mixture. In another bowl combine carrots, apple, and raisins.
3. In a medium bowl combine eggs, oil, milk, and vanilla. Stir in carrot mixture. Add egg mixture all at once to flour mixture. Stir just until moistened (batter should be lumpy). Spoon batter into prepared cups, filling each three-fourths full. If desired, sprinkle with Coconut Streusel.
4. Bake 20 to 25 minutes or until golden. Cool in cups on wire rack 10 minutes. Remove muffins; serve warm or cool. Makes 24 servings.
PER SERVING *161 cal., 7 g fat (1 g sat. fat), 24 mg chol., 172 mg sodium, 23 g carb., 1 g fiber, 2 g pro.*
Coconut Streusel In a bowl combine ¼ cup all-purpose flour and ¼ cup packed brown sugar. Using a pastry blender, cut in ¼ cup cold butter, cut up, until mixture resembles coarse crumbs. Stir in ½ cup shredded coconut.

Festive Desserts

Savor all the sweetness of this most extravagant season. Splurge on holiday cakes, pies, puddings, and cheesecakes.

GLAZED PUMPKIN-
PECAN CAKES,
PAGE 79.

GINGER-CIDER
CHEESECAKE,
PAGE 90

TRIPLE-LAYER HAZELNUT SPICE CAKE

STAND 1 hour
PREP 30 minutes
BAKE 35 minutes at 375°F
COOL 1 hour
COOK 25 minutes
CHILL 30 minutes

2½ cups dried fruit, such as raisins or apricots and/or cherries chopped to the size of raisins
1 cup rum or apple juice
2¾ cups all-purpose flour
2 Tbsp. unsweetened cocoa powder
1 Tbsp. ground cinnamon
1 tsp. kosher salt
1 tsp. baking powder
1 tsp. ground ginger
1 tsp. ground nutmeg
1 tsp. ground allspice
¼ tsp. ground cloves
2¼ cups sugar
1 cup vegetable oil
¼ cup sour cream
2 Tbsp. molasses
3 eggs
1 cup milk
6 oz. hazelnuts (1¼ cups), toasted* and finely chopped
1½ cups unsalted butter (3 sticks), softened
6 cups powdered sugar
1 Tbsp. vanilla
1 recipe Homemade Lemon Curd or ½ cup purchased lemon curd and 1 tsp. lemon zest

1. For the cake, in a medium bowl soak dried fruit in rum at least 1 hour or up to 8 hours.

2. Preheat oven to 375°F. Butter three 8-inch cake pans; line with parchment paper then butter paper.

3. In a medium bowl whisk together flour, cocoa powder, cinnamon, salt, baking powder, ginger, nutmeg, allspice, and cloves.

4. In a large bowl beat sugar, oil, sour cream, and molasses with a mixer on medium-high just until combined. Add eggs, one at a time, beating until combined after each addition. Strain fruit, adding any liquid to batter; set aside fruit.

5. Beat in one-third of the flour mixture just until combined. Add half the milk and mix to combine. Add half the remaining flour mixture then remaining milk, mixing just to combine between additions. Beat in remaining flour until batter is combined and uniform. Fold in hazelnuts and soaked fruit. Pour batter into prepared pans.

6. Bake 35 to 40 minutes or until a wooden toothpick inserted near center comes out with moist crumbs. Cool completely in pans on wire racks. Remove from pans. If desired, wrap and freeze cakes up to 1 month.

7. For buttercream frosting, in an extra-large bowl beat unsalted butter and powdered sugar with a mixer on medium 3 to 4 minutes or until fluffy. (Frosting may appear crumbly at first but will come together.) Beat in vanilla.

8. In a large bowl fold together buttercream frosting and lemon curd. Spread a thick layer between cake layers; frost cake with remaining frosting. Secure cake layers with long skewers, if necessary, until set. Loosely cover and refrigerate up to 1 day. Let stand 1 hour before serving. Makes 18 servings.

Homemade Lemon Curd Remove 1½ tsp. zest and squeeze ⅓ cup juice (2 lemons). In a large heatproof bowl whisk together zest, juice, 4 egg yolks, ⅔ cup sugar, and a pinch of salt. Place a bowl over a saucepan of simmering water (bowl should not touch water). Cook until curd mixture begins to thicken (160°F), 15 to 20 minutes, stirring constantly with a rubber spatula. Add ⅓ cup unsalted butter, cut up; cook and stir 10 to 15 minutes more or until butter is melted and curd is consistency of thick pudding and coats the back of a metal spoon. If there are any lumps, press curd through a fine-mesh sieve. Place plastic wrap on curd surface; chill 30 minutes or up to 3 days. Makes 1 cup.

***Tip** To toast hazelnuts, preheat oven to 350°F. Spread nuts in a shallow baking pan. Bake 8 to 10 minutes or until nuts are lightly toasted. Cool nuts slightly; place on a clean kitchen towel. Rub nuts with towel to remove loose skins.

PER SERVING *814 cal., 39 g fat (13 g sat. fat), 123 mg chol., 122 mg sodium, 108 g carb., 2 g fiber, 7 g pro.*

TRIPLE-LAYER HAZELNUT SPICE CAKE

GLAZED PUMPKIN-PECAN CAKES

PICTURED ON PAGE 76.
PREP 30 minutes
BAKE 30 minutes at 325°F
COOL 10 minutes

1   orange
2   eggs, lightly beaten
1   cup granulated sugar
1   cup water
¾   cup canned pumpkin
¼   cup vegetable oil
2   tsp. vanilla
1   cup all-purpose flour
1   cup whole wheat flour
2½ tsp. baking powder
2   tsp. pumpkin pie spice
½   tsp. salt
¾   cup finely chopped pecans,
    toasted (tip, page 22)
1   cup powdered sugar

1. Preheat oven to 325°F. Generously grease and flour ten 3¾- to 4-inch mini fluted tube pans or one 10-inch fluted tube pan. Remove 2 tsp. zest and squeeze juice from orange. Set juice aside for glaze.
2. In a large bowl combine orange zest and next six ingredients (through vanilla). Stir in flours, baking powder, pumpkin pie spice, and salt until combined.
3. Sprinkle about 1 Tbsp. pecans in each prepared pan then top with about ⅓ cup batter. Or sprinkle pecans in 10-inch pan and top with batter. Bake 30 to 35 minutes for mini cakes, 45 to 50 minutes for 10-inch cake, or until a wooden toothpick inserted in center(s) comes out clean. Cool on a wire rack 10 minutes for mini cakes or 20 minutes for large cake. Remove from pan(s); cool completely on wire rack.
4. Meanwhile, for glaze, in a medium bowl stir together powdered sugar and enough orange juice (3 to 4 tsp.) to make drizzling consistency.
5. Drizzle cake(s) with glaze and, if desired, sprinkle with additional pumpkin pie spice. Makes 10 servings.
PER SERVING *341 cal., 13 g fat (2 g sat. fat), 37 mg chol., 255 mg sodium, 54 g carb., 3 g fiber, 5 g pro.*

BUTTERSCOTCH MARBLE CAKE

BUTTERSCOTCH MARBLE CAKE

PREP 20 minutes
BAKE 55 minutes at 350°F
COOL 2 hours

1   pkg. 2-layer-size white cake mix
1   3.4-oz. pkg. instant butterscotch
    pudding and pie filling mix
1   cup water
4   eggs
¼   cup vegetable oil
½   cup chocolate-flavor syrup
2   oz. sweet baking chocolate,
    chopped
2   Tbsp. butter
¾   cup powdered sugar
1   Tbsp. hot water

1. Preheat oven to 350°F. Grease and flour a 10-inch fluted tube pan.
2. In a large bowl combine cake mix, pudding mix, 1 cup water, eggs, and oil. Beat with a mixer on low just until combined. Beat on medium 2 minutes.
3. Transfer 1½ cups batter to a medium bowl; stir in chocolate syrup. Pour light-color batter into prepared pan. Top with chocolate batter. Using a table knife, gently cut through batters to swirl.
4. Bake 55 to 60 minutes or until a toothpick inserted near center comes out clean. Cool in pan on a wire rack 15 minutes. Remove cake from pan; cool completely on wire rack.
5. For icing, in a small saucepan combine sweet baking chocolate and the butter. Heat and stir over low heat until melted. Remove from heat. Stir in powdered sugar and 1 Tbsp. hot water, 1 tsp. at a time, to make drizzling consistency. Drizzle icing over cake. Makes 12 servings.
PER SERVING *377 cal., 14 g fat (4 g sat. fat), 76 mg chol., 467 mg sodium, 60 g carb., 1 g fiber, 5 g pro.*

SPICE CAKE WITH BROWN SUGAR MERINGUE FROSTING

STAND 30 minutes
PREP 30 minutes
BAKE 30 minutes at 350°F
COOL 1 hour

½	cup butter
2	eggs
2⅔	cups all-purpose flour
⅔	cup granulated sugar
⅔	cup packed brown sugar
1	Tbsp. baking powder
1	tsp. baking soda
1	tsp. freshly grated nutmeg or ½ tsp. ground cinnamon
1⅓	cups milk
2	tsp. vanilla
1	recipe Brown Sugar Meringue Frosting
	Chopped pecans, toasted (tip, page 22) (optional)
	Freshly grated nutmeg (optional)

1. Allow butter and eggs to stand at room temperature 30 minutes. Meanwhile, grease and lightly flour two 8×1½-inch round cake pans.
2. Preheat oven to 350°F. In a large bowl stir together flour, granulated sugar, brown sugar, baking powder, baking soda, and 1 tsp. nutmeg. Add butter, eggs, milk, and vanilla. Beat with a mixer on low until combined. Beat on medium 1 minute. Spoon batter into prepared pans.
3. Bake 30 to 35 minutes or until a toothpick inserted near centers comes out clean. Cool layers in pans on wire racks 10 minutes. Remove from pans; cool completely on wire racks.
4. Place one cake layer, bottom side up, on a serving plate. Spread top with Brown Sugar Meringue Frosting. Top with second layer, top side up. Spread top with remaining frosting, swirling to form high peaks. If desired, use a kitchen torch to brown peaks of frosting. If desired, top with chopped pecans and additional nutmeg. Makes 10 servings.

Brown Sugar Meringue Frosting In the top of a 2-qt. double boiler beat ¾ cup packed brown sugar, 3 Tbsp. cold water, 1 egg white, and ¼ tsp. cream of tartar with a mixer on low 30 seconds. Place over boiling water (upper pan should not touch water). Cook, beating constantly with mixer on high, 10 to 13 minutes or until an instant-read thermometer registers 160°F, occasionally stopping mixer and quickly scraping sides of pan. Remove from heat; add ½ tsp. vanilla. Beat 1 minute or until frosting is fluffy and soft peaks form (tips curl). Makes about 2½ cups.
PER SERVING 411 cal., 11 g fat (6 g sat. fat), 64 mg chol., 398 mg sodium, 72 g carb., 1 g fiber, 6 g pro.

APPLE-MAPLE SPICE CAKE

PREP 35 minutes
BAKE 45 minutes at 350°F
COOL 10 minutes

1½	cups all-purpose flour
½	cup whole wheat flour
2	tsp. baking powder
1½	tsp. ground cinnamon
½	tsp. baking soda
½	tsp. salt
½	tsp. ground nutmeg
⅛	tsp. ground cloves
⅔	cup butter, softened
1	cup granulated sugar
2	eggs, room temperature
1	cup apple butter
¼	cup maple syrup
4	medium gala and/or Granny Smith apples, cored and finely chopped
⅓	cup butter
⅔	cup packed brown sugar
⅓	cup heavy cream
2	Tbsp. maple syrup

1. Preheat oven to 350°F. Butter and flour a 10-inch fluted tube pan. In a medium bowl whisk together the first eight ingredients (through cloves).
2. In a large bowl beat ⅔ cup softened butter with a mixer on medium 30 seconds. Gradually add granulated sugar, ¼ cup at a time, beating on medium until combined. Scrape bowl;

SPICE CAKE WITH BROWN SUGAR MERINGUE FROSTING

APPLE-MAPLE SPICE CAKE

beat 2 minutes more. Add eggs, one at a time, beating after each addition. Beat in apple butter and the ¼ cup maple syrup (batter may appear curdled). Gradually add flour mixture, beating on low until well combined. Fold in half the apples. Spread batter into prepared pan.

3. Bake 45 minutes or until a wooden toothpick inserted in center comes out clean. Cool in pan 10 minutes. Remove from pan; cool slightly on a wire rack.
4. Meanwhile for topping, in a large skillet melt ⅓ cup butter over medium heat. Add remaining apples. Cook and stir 1 to 2 minutes or until softened. Stir in brown sugar and cream. Bring

to boiling, stirring to dissolve sugar. Boil gently, uncovered, 2 to 3 minutes. Remove from heat. Stir in 2 Tbsp. maple syrup. Cool slightly. Spoon over cake. Serve cake warm or at room temperature. Makes 12 servings.
PER SERVING *540 cal., 19 g fat (12 g sat. fat), 79 mg chol., 383 mg sodium, 90 g carb., 4 g fiber, 4 g pro.*

SWEET POTATO-
CHOCOLATE POUND CAKE

SWEET POTATO-CHOCOLATE POUND CAKE

PREP 35 minutes
BAKE 45 minutes at 350°F
COOL 10 minutes
STAND 5 minutes

- 1 10- to 12-oz. sweet potato, scrubbed
- 8 oz. semisweet or bittersweet chocolate, chopped
- 3 cups all-purpose flour
- 2 tsp. pumpkin pie spice
- 1½ tsp. baking powder
- 1½ tsp. salt
- 1 cup butter, softened
- 2 cups sugar
- 5 eggs
- 1 cup sour cream
- 1 Tbsp. vanilla
- ⅔ cup heavy cream
   Flaky sea salt

1. Pierce potato several times with a fork. Microwave on high 5 minutes or until tender. Cool until easy to handle.
2. Halve potato lengthwise. Scrape pulp into a medium bowl. Mash until smooth. Measure ¾ cup (save any remaining mashed sweet potato for another use). In a small microwave-safe bowl heat 2 oz. of the chocolate on high 30 to 45 seconds or until melted, stirring once.
3. Preheat oven to 350°F. Grease and flour two 8-inch loaf pans or coat with nonstick spray for baking. In a medium bowl whisk together flour, pumpkin pie spice, baking powder, and salt. In an extra-large bowl beat butter and sugar on medium-high 2 to 3 minutes or until light and fluffy. Add eggs, one at a time, beating after each addition until combined. Gradually add flour mixture, beating until combined. Beat in sour cream, mashed sweet potato, and vanilla until combined. Transfer 3 cups batter to a medium bowl; stir in melted chocolate.
4. Alternately spoon mounds of each cake batter into prepared pans. Using a knife, swirl batters together. Bake 45 minutes or until toothpick inserted near centers comes out clean. Cool in pans on a wire rack 10 minutes. Remove from pans; cool completely.
5. For ganache, in a small saucepan bring cream just to boiling over medium-high. Remove from heat. Add remaining 6 oz. chopped chocolate (do not stir). Let stand 5 minutes. Stir until smooth. Spoon ganache over cakes. Sprinkle with sea salt flakes. Makes 16 servings.

S'MORES
ICEBOX CAKE

S'MORES ICEBOX CAKE

PREP 20 minutes
CHILL 6 hours
BROIL 1 minute

1½ cups heavy cream
½ 7-oz. carton mascarpone cheese
    or 4 oz. cream cheese
½ cup powdered sugar
2 tsp. vanilla
1 7-oz. jar marshmallow creme
1¼ cups tiny marshmallows
¾ cup miniature semisweet
    chocolate chips
7 to 10 graham cracker rectangles,
    broken into quarters

1. In a large bowl beat cream, mascarpone cheese, powdered sugar, and vanilla with a mixer on medium until soft peaks form (tips curl). Add marshmallow creme; beat until fluffy. Fold in 1 cup of the marshmallows and ½ cup of the chocolate chips.
2. Spread 1 cup cream mixture into a 9×5-inch loaf pan. Spread one graham cracker quarter with a small spoonful of cream mixture. Add a graham cracker on top. Stand sandwiched crackers upright in cream layer. Repeat with remaining crackers and cream. Cover; chill 6 to 24 hours.
3. Preheat broiler. Sprinkle top with remaining ¼ cup marshmallows. Broil 3 to 4 inches from heat 1 minute or until golden. Sprinkle with remaining ¼ cup chocolate chips. Makes 12 servings.
PER SERVING *347 cal., 19 g fat (12 g sat. fat), 46 mg chol., 66 mg sodium, 40 g carb., 0 g fiber, 3 g pro.*

CARAMELIZED PEAR
SKILLET CAKE

CARAMELIZED PEAR SKILLET CAKE

PREP 20 minutes
BAKE 50 minutes at 350°F
COOL 10 minutes

½ cup cold butter
⅔ cup packed light brown sugar
4 Bosc pears, peeled, halved
    lengthwise, and cored
2 cups all-purpose flour
1 tsp. baking powder
1 tsp. ground ginger
¼ tsp. salt
¼ tsp. baking soda
¼ tsp. ground nutmeg
¼ tsp. ground cloves
½ cup butter, softened
2 eggs
½ cup molasses
¾ cup water
1 recipe Bourbon Sauce

1. Place ½ cup cold butter in a 10-inch cast-iron skillet. Place in cold oven; preheat oven to 350°F. Once butter has melted, whisk in ⅓ cup of the brown sugar. Arrange pears, cut sides down, in skillet. Bake 20 to 25 minutes or just until tender and starting to brown. Meanwhile, in a medium bowl whisk together the next seven ingredients (through cloves).
2. In a large bowl beat ½ cup softened butter on medium 30 seconds. Add remaining ⅓ cup brown sugar; beat until combined. Beat in eggs and molasses. Alternately add flour mixture and water to bowl, beating on low after each addition just until combined. Pour batter over pears.
3. Bake 30 to 35 minutes or until a toothpick inserted near center comes out clean. Cool in skillet 10 minutes. Invert onto a serving plate. Drizzle with Bourbon Sauce. Makes 8 servings.
Bourbon Sauce In a small saucepan melt ¼ cup butter over medium. Stir in ½ cup sugar, 1 egg yolk, and 2 Tbsp. water. Cook and stir 6 to 8 minutes or just until boiling. Remove from heat. Stir in 2 Tbsp. bourbon. Cool slightly. Makes ¾ cup.
PER SERVING *640 cal., 31 g fat (19 g sat. fat), 146 mg chol., 435 mg sodium, 85 g carb., 4 g fiber, 6 g pro.*

PUMPKIN BUTTER-OATMEAL PIE

PUMPKIN BUTTER-OATMEAL PIE

PREP 40 minutes
BAKE 12 minutes at 450°F/45 minutes at 350°F

1   **recipe Pastry for Double-Crust Pie**
1   **egg, lightly beaten**
½   **cup butter**
⅔   **cup regular rolled oats**
½   **cup light-color corn syrup**
2   **eggs**
1   **9-oz. jar pumpkin butter**
¾   **cup canned pumpkin**
1   **tsp. vanilla**
½   **tsp. ground cinnamon**
¼   **tsp. ground nutmeg**
⅛   **tsp. salt**
1   **recipe Sweetened Whipped Cream or vanilla ice cream (optional)**

1. Preheat oven to 450°F. Prepare pastry. On a lightly floured surface, roll half the pastry into a 12-inch circle. Line a 9-inch pie plate with pastry. Trim pastry even with edge of pie plate.
2. Roll remaining pastry half to ⅛-inch thickness. Cut ¾- to 1-inch shapes with cookie cutters. For egg wash, stir together beaten egg and 1 Tbsp. water. Brush edge of pastry with egg wash; arrange cutouts around edge. Brush cutouts with egg wash. Do not prick pastry. Line pastry with a double thickness of foil. Bake 8 minutes. Remove foil. Bake 4 to 5 minutes more or until crust is set and dry. Remove from oven. Reduce oven temperature to 350°F.
3. Meanwhile, for filling, in a skillet cook 1 Tbsp. of the butter over low heat until golden brown; add oats. Cook and stir 3 to 4 minutes or until toasted; cool.
4. In a large microwave-safe bowl heat remaining butter 30 to 45 seconds or

until melted. Stir in corn syrup; whisk in 2 eggs, pumpkin butter, pumpkin, vanilla, cinnamon, nutmeg, and salt. Stir in oats. Pour filling into crust.
5. Cover edge of pie with foil to prevent overbrowning. Bake 45 to 50 minutes or until filling is set. Cool on a wire rack. If desired, serve with Sweetened Whipped Cream. Makes 8 servings.
Pastry for Double-Crust Pie In a large bowl stir together 2½ cups flour and 1 tsp. salt. Using a pastry blender, cut in ½ cup shortening and ¼ cup cut-up butter until pieces are pea size. Sprinkle 1 Tbsp. ice water over part of the flour mixture; toss gently with a fork. Push moistened pastry to side of bowl. Repeat moistening flour mixture, with 1 Tbsp. water at a time, until flour mixture is moistened (¼ to ⅓ cup ice water total). Gather into a ball, knead gently until pastry holds together.
PER SERVING *594 cal., 33 g fat (15 g sat. fat), 116 mg chol., 551 mg sodium, 68 g carb., 2 g fiber, 8 g pro.*
Sweetened Whipped Cream In a medium chilled bowl beat 1 cup heavy cream, 2 Tbsp. sugar, and ½ tsp. vanilla with a mixer on medium until soft peaks form (tips curl).

SPICED SUGAR CREAM PIE

PREP 25 minutes
BAKE 50 minutes at 350°F
CHILL 2 hours

1   **recipe Nut Pastry Shell**
¾   **cup packed brown sugar**
⅓   **cup all-purpose flour**
¼   **cup granulated sugar**
½   **tsp. freshly grated nutmeg or ¼ tsp. ground nutmeg**
½   **tsp. ground cinnamon**

Dash **ground cloves (optional)**
2½ **cups heavy cream**
1   **vanilla bean, split lengthwise, or 1 tsp. vanilla**
1   **recipe Sugar Sprinkle (optional)**

1. Make Nut Pastry Shell. Preheat oven to 350°F. For filling, in a large bowl combine brown sugar, flour, granulated sugar, nutmeg, cinnamon, and, if desired, cloves, breaking up clumps of brown sugar. Slowly whisk cream into sugar mixture. If using, scrape seeds from vanilla bean. Whisk vanilla bean seeds or vanilla into sugar mixture.
2. Pour filling into shell. To prevent overbrowning, cover edge with foil. Place on center oven rack.
3. Bake 25 minutes; remove foil. Bake 25 to 30 minutes more or until top is lightly browned and filling is bubbly across surface (pie won't appear set but will firm up upon cooling). Cool completely on a wire rack.
4. Cover; chill within 2 hours. Chill 2 to 24 hours or until set. If desired, just before serving cut pie and use a fine-mesh sieve to sift Sugar Sprinkle over pie. Makes 8 servings.
Nut Pastry Shell In a medium bowl stir together 1¼ cups all-purpose flour, ¼ cup finely ground pecans, and ½ tsp. salt. Using a pastry blender, cut in ¼ cup shortening and ¼ cup butter until pieces are pea size. Sprinkle 1 Tbsp. ice water over part of the flour mixture; toss gently with a fork. Push moistened dough to side of bowl. Repeat with additional ice water, 1 Tbsp. at a time (¼ to ⅓ cup total), until all of the flour mixture is moistened. Gather pastry into a ball; knead gently until pastry holds together. On a lightly floured surface, slightly flatten pastry with hands. Roll pastry from center to edge into a 12-inch circle. Wrap around rolling pin; unroll into a 9-inch pie plate. Ease pastry without stretching into pie plate it. Trim pastry ½ inch beyond edge of pie plate. Fold under pastry even with plate edge. Crimp as desired. Do not prick pastry.
PER SERVING *584 cal., 42 g fat (23 g sat. fat), 118 mg chol., 221 mg sodium, 48 g carb., 1 g fiber, 5 g pro.*
Sugar Sprinkle In a small bowl combine 1 Tbsp. powdered sugar, a dash of ground nutmeg, and a dash of cinnamon.

SPICED SUGAR
CREAM PIE

GINGER PEAR
GALETTE

GINGER PEAR GALETTE

PREP 25 minutes
BAKE 25 minutes at 400°F

½ 17.3-oz. pkg. frozen puff pastry sheets, thawed (1 sheet)
1 egg white, lightly beaten
2 Tbsp. all-purpose flour
2 Tbsp. granulated sugar
2 Tbsp. packed brown sugar
1 Tbsp. finely chopped crystallized ginger
1 tsp. lemon zest
2 Tbsp. butter
3 large pears, peeled and thinly sliced
   Sweetened Whipped Cream (recipe, page 84) (optional)

1. Preheat oven to 400°F. Line a baking sheet with parchment paper; set aside. On a lightly floured surface, unfold pastry. Roll into a 14×11-inch rectangle; trim to a 12×10-inch rectangle. Place on prepared baking sheet. Brush edges of pastry with egg white. Cut ½-inch strips from pastry trimmings. Place strips on edges of pastry rectangle, pressing to form raised rim; trim ends. Brush edges with egg white. Prick center of pastry rectangle with a fork.
2. For topping, in a bowl stir together flour, granulated sugar, brown sugar, crystallized ginger, and lemon zest. Cut in butter until pieces are pea size.
3. Sprinkle half the topping on pastry. Arrange pear slices, overlapping slightly. Sprinkle with remaining topping.
4. Bake 25 minutes or until pastry is golden and pears are tender. If desired, top with Sweetened Whipped Cream. Serve warm. Makes 8 servings.
PER SERVING *282 cal., 15 g fat (5 g sat. fat), 8 mg chol., 106 mg sodium, 36 g carb., 3 g fiber, 3 g pro.*

SPICED APPLE TARTE TATIN

PREP 30 minutes
COOK 20 minutes
BAKE 20 minutes at 400°F
COOL 20 minutes

1 14-oz. pkg. (1 sheet) frozen all-butter puff pastry or regular puff pastry, thawed
4 large Braeburn apples (2 lb.)
¼ cup butter
½ cup sugar

SPICED APPLE TARTE TATIN

¾ tsp. Chinese five-spice powder
¼ tsp. kosher salt

1. Preheat oven to 400°F. Unfold puff pastry onto parchment paper. (If package has two sheets, unfold both and layer together.) Roll pastry into an 11-inch square, then cut an 11-inch circle. Cover with plastic wrap and chill until needed.
2. Peel apples. Working from top to bottom, cut three slices from rounded sides of each apple. In a 10-inch cast-iron skillet melt butter over medium heat. Sprinkle with sugar. Add a single layer of apple slices, cut sides down. Cut remaining slices into thirds and tuck around apples in skillet. Cook

over medium-high heat 3 minutes or until liquid is bubbly and light golden. Cook over medium heat 4 minutes. Sprinkle with five-spice powder and salt. Turn apple slices, rounded sides down; cook 1 minute more or until liquid is thickened and deep golden brown. Cool 10 minutes.
3. Cover apples with pastry, tucking edges into skillet. Cut two slits in pastry. Bake 20 to 25 minutes or until pastry is golden. Cool on a wire rack 10 minutes. Quickly invert tart onto a platter. Makes 8 servings.
PER SERVING *369 cal., 22 g fat (14 g sat. fat), 59 mg chol., 274 mg sodium, 42 g carb., 3 g fiber, 3 g pro.*

CINNAMON ROLL-APPLE PIE COBBLER

PREP 30 minutes
BAKE 1 hour 15 minutes at 350°F
COOL 30 minutes

- ½ cup sugar
- 2 Tbsp. all-purpose flour
- 1 tsp. ground ginger
- 7 cups peeled, cored, and sliced Braeburn, Piñata, Granny Smith, Idared, and/or Golden Delicious apples
- ¼ cup golden raisins
- ¼ cup water
- 1 17.5-oz. pkg. (5) refrigerated large cinnamon rolls with icing, quartered

1. Preheat oven to 350°F. In an extra-large bowl stir together sugar, flour, and ginger. Add apples, raisins, and water; toss to combine. Spoon apple mixture into a 2-qt. casserole;* cover. Place a foil-lined baking sheet on the rack below cobbler. Bake, covered, 50 minutes or just until apples begin to soften.

2. Arrange cinnamon roll pieces on apple filling. Bake, uncovered, 25 to 30 minutes or until rolls are golden. Cool at least 30 minutes. Drizzle icing from cinnamon roll package on rolls. Makes 8 servings.

*Tip Or use a 2-qt. square baking dish. Prepare as directed, covering dish with foil and reducing baking time to 40 minutes in Step 1. Continue as directed in Step 2.

PER SERVING *316 cal., 6 g fat (1 g sat. fat), 0 mg chol., 409 mg sodium, 65 g carb., 3 g fiber, 3 g pro.*

APPLE DUTCH BABY

PREP 20 minutes
BAKE 15 minutes at 425°F

- 3 eggs, lightly beaten
- ½ cup milk
- ½ cup all-purpose flour
- 1 Tbsp. granulated sugar
- ½ tsp. vanilla
- ¼ tsp. salt
- ¼ tsp. ground cinnamon
- 3 Tbsp. butter
- 1⅓ cups thinly sliced red cooking apple
- 2 Tbsp. packed brown sugar
- 2 Tbsp. pure maple syrup

1. Preheat oven to 425°F. In a medium bowl combine eggs and milk. Stir in the next five ingredients (through cinnamon) until smooth.

2. In a 9- or 10-inch cast-iron skillet melt 1½ Tbsp. of the butter over medium heat. Pour batter into skillet. Bake 15 minutes or until light brown and puffed.

3. While Dutch Baby bakes, in a medium saucepan melt remaining 1½ Tbsp. butter over medium-high. Add apple; cook 5 minutes or until crisp-tender and brown on edges, stirring occasionally. Stir in brown sugar and maple syrup. Cook 2 to 3 minutes more or until apple is tender. Serve Dutch Baby topped with cooked apples. Makes 4 servings.

PER SERVING *287 cal., 13 g fat (7 g sat. fat), 165 mg chol., 285 mg sodium, 35 g carb., 1 g fiber, 8 g pro.*

CINNAMON ROLL APPLE PIE COBBLER

COFFEE AND CREAM BREAD PUDDINGS

PREP 25 minutes
BAKE 30 minutes at 375°F
COOL 10 minutes

- 2 **cups milk**
- ¼ **cup heavy cream**
- 2 **Tbsp. instant coffee crystals**
- 6 **eggs, lightly beaten**
- ⅔ **cup granulated sugar**
- ⅓ **cup packed brown sugar**
- 2 **tsp. vanilla**
- 8 **cups torn French or Italian bread (9 to 10 oz.)**
- 1 **recipe Cream Cheese Topping**
  Chocolate-covered coffee beans, chopped (optional)

1. Preheat oven to 375°F. Grease six 3½-inch muffin cups; set aside.
2. In a large bowl combine milk, cream, and coffee crystals, stirring until coffee is dissolved. Stir in eggs, granulated sugar, brown sugar, and vanilla. Stir in torn bread until moistened. Spoon bread mixture into prepared muffin cups, filling each about three-fourths full.
3. Bake 30 minutes or until puffed and set and a knife inserted in centers comes out clean. Cool in muffin cups on a wire rack 10 minutes (puddings will fall as they cool).
4. Using two small serving spoons, remove puddings from muffin cups. Spoon about 3 rounded Tbsp. Cream Cheese Topping onto each pudding. If desired, sprinkle with chopped coffee beans. Makes 6 servings.
Cream Cheese Topping In a medium bowl beat 1 oz. softened cream cheese and 1 Tbsp. powdered sugar with a mixer on medium until smooth. Gradually add ¾ cup heavy cream, beating until combined. Beat on medium until soft peaks form (tips curl). Makes about 1½ cups.
PER SERVING *538 cal., 24 g fat (13 g sat. fat), 253 mg chol., 362 mg sodium, 67 g carb., 1 g fiber, 15 g pro.*

COFFEE AND CREAM BREAD PUDDINGS

APPLE DUTCH BABY

BANANA-FIG SKILLET CRISP

BANANA-FIG SKILLET CRISP

START TO FINISH 30 minutes

¼ cup regular rolled oats
¼ cup chopped raw macadamia nuts
2 Tbsp. shredded or flaked coconut
2 Tbsp. granulated sugar
1½ Tbsp. butter
⅛ tsp. ground ginger
¼ cup butter
3 medium bananas, cut into ½-inch pieces
½ cup dried calimyrna or Kalamata figs, snipped
¼ cup packed brown sugar
1 tsp. grated fresh ginger or ¼ tsp. ground ginger
¼ tsp. ground cinnamon
2 Tbsp. honey
2 Tbsp. rum or water
1½ cups vanilla or coconut ice cream

1. For topping, in a 9-inch cast-iron skillet cook oats and macadamia nuts over medium 2 to 3 minutes or until nuts are very light brown, stirring frequently. Add coconut; cook and stir 2 to 3 minutes more or until mixture is toasted. Stir in granulated sugar, 1½ Tbsp. butter, and ⅛ tsp. ginger until butter is melted. Transfer to a bowl.
2. In the same skillet melt ¼ cup butter over medium heat. Add bananas,

figs, brown sugar, fresh ginger, and cinnamon; cook 3 to 5 minutes or just until fruit is softened, stirring occasionally. Carefully stir in honey and rum; cook 1 minute more.
3. Sprinkle topping over fruit mixture in skillet. Serve warm topped with ice cream. Makes 4 servings.
PER SERVING *694 cal., 37 g fat (20 g sat. fat), 116 mg chol., 201 mg sodium, 87 g carb., 6 g fiber, 6 g pro.*

GINGER-CIDER CHEESECAKE

PREP 20 minutes
BAKE 45 minutes at 350°F
COOL 45 minutes
CHILL 3 hours
COOK 25 minutes

42 gingersnap cookies
1 Tbsp. granulated sugar
¼ cup butter, melted
3 8-oz. pkg. cream cheese, softened
¾ cup granulated sugar
½ cup packed brown sugar
3 Tbsp. all-purpose flour
1½ cups apple cider
3 eggs, lightly beaten
¼ cup finely chopped candied ginger
2 Tbsp. grated fresh ginger
1 cup cranberries
Sage leaves (optional)

1. Preheat oven to 350°F. For crust, place 30 cookies in a food processor; cover and process until fine. Add 1 Tbsp. sugar and butter; process until combined. Press mixture onto the bottom and 1½ inches up the sides of a 9-inch springform pan.
2. For filling, in a large bowl beat cream cheese, ½ cup of the sugar, the brown sugar, and flour with a mixer until smooth. Beat in ½ cup of the cider just until combined. Stir in eggs, candied ginger, and fresh ginger. Pour into crust-lined pan. Arrange remaining 12 gingersnap cookies on the filling. Place on a rimmed baking sheet. Bake 45 to 50 minutes or until edges puff and center and is almost set.
3. Cool in pan on a wire rack 15 minutes. Use a knife to loosen sides of cheesecake from sides of pan. Cool 30 minutes more. Remove sides of pan. Cool completely. Cover and chill 3 to 4 hours before serving.
4. For glaze, place remaining 1 cup cider, cranberries, and remaining ¼ cup sugar in a small saucepan. Bring to boiling, stirring to dissolve sugar; reduce heat. Boil gently, uncovered, 25 minutes or until syrupy. Cool completely. Spoon over cheesecake and, if desired, top with sage. Makes 12 servings.
PER SERVING *463 cal., 27 g fat (14 g sat. fat), 119 mg chol., 369 mg sodium, 51 g carb., 1 g fiber, 6 g pro.*

GINGER-CIDER
CHEESECAKE

BUTTERSCOTCH PUDDING WITH CRÈME FRAÎCHE TOPPING

SALTED CARAMEL POTS DE CRÈME

PREP 35 minutes
BAKE 40 minutes at 325°F
COOL 30 minutes
CHILL 4 hours

1¼   cups sugar
¼   cup water
¼   tsp. salt
1½   cups heavy cream
½   cup whole milk
6   egg yolks
1   tsp. fleur de sel or other flaked
    sea salt

1. Preheat oven to 325°F. Position oven rack at center of oven. Place eight 4-oz. pots de crème dishes or ramekins or eight 6-oz. custard cups in a large roasting pan.
2. In a medium saucepan combine sugar, water, and ¼ tsp. salt. Heat and stir over low heat until sugar is dissolved. Using a soft pastry brush dipped in water, brush down any sugar crystals on sides of saucepan. Increase heat to medium-high; bring mixture to boiling. Boil, without stirring, 8 to 10 minutes or until mixture turns amber in color. Remove from heat.
3. Whisking constantly, carefully add cream and milk in a slow stream (mixture will steam and sugar will harden). Return to heat. Cook and whisk about 2 minutes or until sugar has dissolved.
4. In a large bowl whisk egg yolks until light and foamy. Slowly whisk cream mixture into beaten egg yolks. Pour mixture through a fine-mesh sieve into a 4-cup glass measure with pouring spout. Divide mixture among pots.
5. Add hot water to the roasting pan to halfway up the sides of the dishes. Carefully place pan on center oven rack. Bake 40 minutes or until edges are set and centers jiggle slightly when shaken. Transfer dishes to wire racks; cool 30 minutes. Cover with plastic wrap. Chill at least 4 hours or up to 24 hours.
6. Before serving, sprinkle a little fleur de sel on each custard. Makes 8 servings.
PER SERVING 327 cal., 21 g fat (12 g sat. fat), 221 mg chol., 302 mg sodium, 34 g carb., 0 g fiber, 3 g pro.

BUTTERSCOTCH PUDDING WITH CRÈME FRAÎCHE TOPPING

PREP 30 minutes
CHILL 4 hours

1   cup packed light brown sugar
¼   cup cornstarch
¼   tsp. salt
4   cups half-and-half or light cream
5   egg yolks, lightly beaten
¼   cup butter, cut into small pieces
2   tsp. vanilla
1   recipe Crème Fraîche Topping

1. In a medium saucepan combine brown sugar, cornstarch, and salt. Stir in half-and-half. Cook and stir over medium heat until mixture is thickened and bubbly. Cook and stir 2 minutes more.
2. Gradually stir about 1 cup hot mixture into egg yolks. Return egg yolk mixture to saucepan. Bring to a gentle boil; reduce heat. Cook and stir 2 minutes. Remove from heat. Stir in butter and vanilla. Pour pudding into a large bowl. Cover surface with plastic wrap. Chill 4 to 5 hours or until well chilled. Serve with Crème Fraîche Topping. Makes 8 servings.

Crème Fraîche Topping In a small serving bowl combine 2 Tbsp. goat cheese, ½ cup crème fraîche, and 1 Tbsp. sugar. Sprinkle lightly with freshly grated nutmeg.
PER SERVING 429 cal., 29 fat (17 g sat. fat), 212 mg chol., 194 mg sodium, 38 g carb., 0 g fiber, 6 g pro.

SALTED CARAMEL
POTS DE CRÈME

Impressive Cookies and Bars

Sweeten the season with platters of homemade cookies, bars, and no-bake treats. Have as much fun making them as you will in sharing them.

SUGAR COOKIES,
PAGE 104

95

BLACK AND
WHITE COOKIES

BLACK-AND-WHITE COOKIES

PREP 45 minutes
CHILL 2 hours
BAKE 7 minutes per batch at 350°F

2½ cups all-purpose flour
1 tsp. baking soda
1 tsp. salt
⅔ cup butter, softened
1 cup granulated sugar
2 eggs
4 tsp. clear vanilla
½ cup buttermilk
4 cups powdered sugar
4 Tbsp. milk
2 Tbsp. light-color corn syrup
3 Tbsp. unsweetened cocoa powder

1. In a medium bowl stir together flour, baking soda, and salt. In a large bowl beat butter with a mixer on medium 30 seconds. Add granulated sugar and beat on medium to high 1 minute, scraping bowl as needed. Beat in eggs and 2 tsp. of the vanilla. Alternately add flour mixture and buttermilk, beating on low after each addition just until combined. Cover and chill 2 hours.
2. Preheat oven to 350°F. Line a cookie sheet with parchment paper. Drop dough by tablespoons 2 inches apart onto prepared cookie sheet (dough will be sticky). Using floured fingers, flatten mounds to 2-inch circles.
3. Bake 7 to 10 minutes or until edges are firm and light brown. Cool on cookie sheet 5 minutes. Remove; cool on a wire rack.
4. For white icing, in a medium bowl stir together powdered sugar, 3 Tbsp. of the milk, the corn syrup, and remaining 2 tsp. vanilla. For chocolate icing, transfer half the mixture to another medium bowl. Stir in cocoa powder and remaining 1 Tbsp. milk. If needed for either icing, stir in additional milk, ½ tsp. at a time, to reach thick glazing consistency.
5. Spread half of each cookie with white icing. Spread remaining half with chocolate icing. Let stand until icings are set. Makes 28 servings.
PER SERVING *190 cal., 5 g fat (3 g sat. fat), 25 mg chol., 179 mg sodium, 35 g carb., 0 g fiber, 2 g pro.*

MACADAMIA-CRANBERRY JUMBLES

PREP 40 minutes
BAKE 7 minutes per batch at 350°F
COOL 1 minute

½ cup shortening
½ cup butter, softened
1½ cups packed brown sugar
1 tsp. baking soda
½ tsp. salt
2 eggs
2 tsp. vanilla
1⅔ cups all-purpose flour
1¼ cups regular or quick-cooking rolled oats, finely ground*
1 cup flaked coconut, toasted**
1 cup white baking chips or semisweet chocolate chips
¾ cup chopped macadamia nuts
¾ cup dried cranberries or tart cherries, chopped

1. Preheat oven to 350°F. In an extra-large bowl beat shortening and butter with a mixer on medium 30 seconds. Add brown sugar, baking soda, and salt and beat until combined, scraping bowl as needed. Beat in eggs and vanilla. Beat in flour and ground oats on low just until combined. Stir in remaining ingredients.
2. Drop dough by small (2 tsp.) scoops*** 2 inches apart onto an ungreased cookie sheet. Bake 7 to 8 minutes or until light brown. Cool on cookie sheet 1 minute. Transfer to a wire rack to cool. Makes 80 servings.
*Tip Place oats in a food processor. Cover and pulse until finely ground. Measure 1 cup ground oats.
**Tip To toast coconut, preheat oven to 350°F. Spread coconut in a shallow baking pan. Bake 5 to 10 minutes or just until lightly browned around edges, watching carefully to prevent burning.
PER SERVING *87 cal., 5 g fat (2 g sat. fat), 8 mg chol., 47 mg sodium, 10 g carb., 0 g fiber, 1 g pro.*
***Tip To make 46 medium cookies, use a 1½-Tbsp. scoop and bake as directed. To make 26 large cookies, use a 3-Tbsp. scoop and bake 10 minutes.

SALTY CARAMEL AND PECAN OATMEAL COOKIES

PREP 30 minutes
BAKE 11 minutes per batch at 350°F

- 1 cup butter, softened
- 1 cup granulated sugar
- 1 cup packed dark brown sugar
- 1 tsp. salt
- 1 tsp. baking powder
- 1 tsp. ground cinnamon
- ½ tsp. baking soda
- 2 eggs
- 2 tsp. vanilla
- 1½ cups all-purpose flour
- 3 cups rolled oats
- 1 11-oz. pkg. caramel baking bits
- 1 cup pecans, toasted and coarsely chopped (tip, page 22)
   Coarse sea salt

1. Preheat oven to 350°F. Line two cookie sheets with parchment paper. In a large bowl beat butter with a mixer on medium to high 30 seconds. Add sugars, salt, baking powder, cinnamon, and baking soda. Beat until combined. Beat in eggs and vanilla until combined. Beat in as much of the flour as you can with the mixer. Stir in remaining flour. Stir in oats, caramel baking bits, and pecans.

2. Drop dough from a small ice cream scoop 2 inches apart onto prepared cookie sheets. Sprinkle with coarse sea salt.

3. Bake 11 to 13 minutes or until edges are light brown (centers will appear undercooked). Cool on cookie sheets 3 to 4 minutes. Transfer to a wire rack to cool. Makes 48 servings.

PER SERVING *145 cal., 7 g fat (3 g sat. fat), 18 mg chol., 421 mg sodium, 21 g carb., 1 g fiber, 2 g pro.*

MACADAMIA-CRANBERRY JUMBLES

SALTY CARAMEL AND PECAN OATMEAL COOKIES

MALTED BUTTER RICHES

PREP 15 minutes
CHILL 1 hour
BAKE 9 minutes per batch at 350°F

- 2 cups all-purpose flour
- ⅔ cup malted milk powder
- 1 tsp. baking soda
- 1 tsp. salt
- ¾ cup unsalted butter, softened
- ¼ cup shortening
- ¾ cup packed light brown sugar
- 1 Tbsp. vanilla
- 1 egg
- 1 egg yolk
- ¾ cup unsalted butter
- 4 cups powdered sugar
- 1 cup malted milk powder
- ½ tsp. salt
- 2 tsp. vanilla
- ½ to ⅔ cup heavy cream
  Whole or crushed malted milk balls (optional)

1. For cookies, line two cookie sheets with parchment paper. In a medium bowl whisk together flour, ⅔ cup malted milk powder, baking soda, and 1 tsp. salt.
2. In a large bowl beat softened butter, shortening, brown sugar, and vanilla on medium 2 minutes or until fluffy. Add egg and egg yolk. Beat on low until combined. Add dry ingredients. Beat on low until some streaks of flour remain. Stir by hand until combined.
3. Using a small cookie scoop or 1-tablespoon measure, scoop dough and roll into 1¼-inch balls. Place 2 inches apart on prepared cookie sheets. Cover with plastic wrap. Chill 1 hour or up to 2 days.
4. Preheat oven to 350°F. Bake cookies 9 to 11 minutes or until light brown. Cool on a wire rack.
5. Meanwhile, for malted brown butter frosting, in a medium saucepan heat ¾ cup butter over medium-high 5 minutes or until butter smells nutty and browned bits begin to form on bottom of pan. Remove from heat; cool slightly. In a large bowl combine powdered sugar, 1 cup malted milk powder, and ½ tsp. salt. Add browned butter (and bits) and vanilla. Stir in enough cream to reach spreadable consistency. Spread frosting on cooled cookies. If desired, top with crushed malted milk balls. Makes 36 servings.
PER SERVING *214 cal., 11 g fat (6 g sat. fat), 36 mg chol., 163 mg sodium, 27 g carb., 0 g fiber, 2 g pro.*

MALTED BUTTER RICHES

OATMEAL-WALNUT-CHOCOLATE CHIP COOKIES

PREP 25 minutes
BAKE 9 minutes per batch at 375°F
COOL 1 minute

- 2½ cups regular rolled oats
- 2 cups all-purpose flour
- 1 tsp. baking powder
- 1 tsp. baking soda
- ½ tsp. salt
- 1 cup butter, softened
- 1 cup granulated sugar
- 1 cup packed brown sugar
- 2 eggs
- 1 tsp. vanilla
- 1 12-oz. pkg. semisweet chocolate pieces (2 cups)
- 1½ cups chopped walnuts or pecans
- 4 oz. milk chocolate bar, grated

OATMEAL-WALNUT
CHOCOLATE CHIP
COOKIES

1. Preheat oven to 375°F. In a medium bowl combine oats, flour, baking powder, baking soda, and salt. Set aside.

2. In a large bowl beat butter with a mixer on medium to high 30 seconds. Add granulated sugar and brown sugar. Beat on medium until combined, scraping sides of bowl occasionally. Beat in eggs and vanilla until combined. Beat in as much flour mixture as you can with mixer. Stir in remaining flour mixture until combined. Stir in chocolate pieces, nuts, and grated chocolate.

3. Drop dough from a large cookie scoop (3 Tbsp.) 4 inches apart onto ungreased cookie sheets. Bake 9 to 10 minutes or until edges are light brown. Cool on cookie sheets 1 minute. Cool on wire racks. Makes 30 servings.

PER SERVING *307 cal., 16 g fat (6 g sat. fat), 31 mg chol., 149 mg sodium, 39 g carb., 3 g fiber, 5 g pro.*

CINNAMON-SUGAR SANDWICH COOKIES WITH DULCE DE LECHE FILLING

CINNAMON-SUGAR SANDWICH COOKIES WITH DULCE DE LECHE FILLING

PREP 45 minutes
BAKE 8 minutes per batch at 350°F

1   cup butter, softened
1½ cups sugar
1   tsp. baking soda
1   tsp. cream of tartar
¼   tsp. salt
2   eggs
1   tsp. vanilla
3   cups all-purpose flour
½   cup sugar
1   Tbsp. ground cinnamon
⅔   cup canned dulce de leche

1. Preheat oven to 350°F. In a large bowl beat butter with a mixer on medium 30 seconds. Add 1½ cups sugar, baking soda, cream of tartar, and salt. Beat until combined, scraping bowl as needed. Beat in eggs and vanilla. Beat in as much flour as you can; stir in any remaining flour.

2. In a small bowl stir together ½ cup sugar and cinnamon. Shape dough into ¾-inch balls. Roll balls in cinnamon-sugar to coat. Place 2 inches apart on ungreased cookie sheets.

3. Bake 8 to 10 minutes or until bottoms are light brown. Remove; cool on a wire rack. Spread about 1 tsp. dulce de leche on bottoms of half the cookies. Top with remaining cookies, bottom sides down. Makes 28 servings.

To Store Layer unfilled cookies between waxed paper in an airtight container. Store at room temperature up to 3 days or freeze up to 3 months. To serve, thaw cookies if frozen. Fill as directed.

PER SERVING *192 cal., 8 g fat (5 g sat. fat), 33 mg chol., 133 mg sodium, 29 g carb., 0 g fiber, 2 g pro.*

CHOCOLATE BLOSSOMS

PREP 25 minutes
BAKE 8 minutes per batch at 350°F

4   oz. bittersweet chocolate, chopped
¾   cup shortening
¼   cup butter, softened
¾   cup granulated sugar
½   cup packed brown sugar
1   Tbsp. instant espresso coffee powder or instant coffee crystals
1   tsp. baking powder
¼   tsp. salt
⅛   tsp. baking soda
1   egg
1   tsp. vanilla
2   cups all-purpose flour
    Milk chocolate stars

1. In a small saucepan heat chopped chocolate over low until melted, stirring occasionally. (Or heat chopped chocolate in a microwave-safe bowl 1 to 1½ minutes or until melted and smooth, stirring twice.) Cool.

2. Meanwhile, preheat oven to 350°F. In a large bowl beat shortening and butter with a mixer on medium 30 seconds. Add ½ cup of the granulated sugar and the next five ingredients (through baking soda). Beat until combined, scraping bowl as needed. Beat in egg and vanilla until combined. Beat in melted chocolate. Beat in flour.

3. Shape dough into 1-inch balls. Roll balls in remaining ¼ cup granulated sugar to coat. Place 2 inches apart on ungreased cookie sheets. Bake 8 to 10 minutes or until edges are firm and bottoms are light brown. Immediately press chocolate stars into cookie centers. Cool cookies on a wire rack. Makes 66 servings.

PER SERVING *92 cal., 5 g fat (2 g sat. fat), 6 mg chol., 30 mg sodium, 11 g carb., 0 g fiber, 1 g pro.*

CHOCOLATE BLOSSOMS

CRANBERRY-ALMOND ICEBOX COOKIES

PREP 25 minutes
CHILL 2 hours
BAKE 8 minutes per batch at 350°F

⅔ cup butter, softened
1 8-oz. can almond paste
¼ cup sugar
1 tsp. baking powder
¼ tsp. salt
¼ cup refrigerated or frozen egg product, thawed, or 1 egg
2 tsp. orange zest (optional)
2 cups all-purpose flour
⅓ cup dried cranberries, finely chopped
¼ cup toasted almonds, finely chopped (tip, page 22)
1 recipe Orange Glaze (optional)

1. In a large bowl beat butter with a mixer on medium 30 seconds. Add almond paste, sugar, baking powder, and salt; beat until well combined. Beat in egg and orange zest (if using). Beat in as much flour as you can. Stir in any remaining flour, cranberries, and almonds.
2. Divide dough in half. Shape each dough portion into an 8-inch log. Wrap logs in plastic wrap. Chill 2 hours or until firm enough to slice.
3. Preheat oven to 350°F. Cut logs into ¼-inch slices. Place slices 1 inch apart on ungreased cookie sheets.
4. Bake 8 to 10 minutes or until edges are firm and centers are set. Transfer cookies to a wire rack to cool. Makes 48 servings.
PER SERVING *73 cal., 4 g fat (2 g sat. fat), 7 mg chol., 45 mg sodium, 8 g carb., 0 g fiber, 1 g pro.*
Orange Glaze In a small bowl stir together ½ cup powdered sugar and ¼ tsp. orange zest. Stir in enough orange juice or milk (2 to 3 tsp. total) to make a drizzling consistency.

**CRANBERRY-ALMOND
ICEBOX COOKIES**

CITRUS MELTAWAYS

CITRUS MELTAWAYS

PREP 30 minutes
CHILL 3 hours
BAKE 12 minutes per batch at 325°F
COOL 4 minutes

¾ cup butter, softened
⅓ cup powdered sugar
2 tsp. orange, lime, and/or lemon zest
3 Tbsp. orange, lime, and/or lemon juice
1 tsp. vanilla
1¾ cups all-purpose flour
2 Tbsp. cornstarch

½ tsp. salt
2 cups powdered sugar

1. In a large bowl beat butter with a mixer on medium 30 seconds. Add ⅓ cup powdered sugar, citrus zest and juice, and vanilla. Beat until combined, scraping bowl as needed. Beat in flour, cornstarch, and salt.
2. Divide dough in half. Shape each half into a 10-inch log. Wrap each in plastic wrap or waxed paper. Chill 3 hours or until firm enough to slice.
3. Preheat oven to 325°F. Line cookie sheets with parchment paper. Using a sharp, thin-blade knife, cut logs into

¼-inch slices. Place 2 inches apart on prepared cookie sheets. Bake 12 to 15 minutes or just until bottoms are golden. Cool on cookie sheets 4 minutes.
4. Place 2 cups powdered sugar in a large bowl. Add warm cookies, two or three at a time, and toss gently to coat. Cool on a wire rack. Makes 80 servings.
Make Ahead Shape dough into logs, wrap in plastic wrap, and freeze up to 2 months. To bake, thaw logs slightly. Slice, then bake 15 to 18 minutes.
PER SERVING *40 cal., 2 g fat (1 g sat. fat), 5 mg chol., 28 mg sodium, 6 g carb., 0 g fiber, 0 g pro.*

PEANUT BUTTER AND JELLY TRIANGLES

PEANUT BUTTER AND JELLY TRIANGLES

PREP 40 minutes
BAKE 8 minutes per batch at 350°F
COOL 2 minutes

1   cup butter, softened
1   cup creamy peanut butter*
1   cup packed brown sugar
½   cup granulated sugar
1½ tsp. baking powder
1   egg
2   egg yolks
1   tsp. vanilla
2½ cups all-purpose flour
1   12-oz. jar cherry jam or preserves
½   cup dried tart cherries, chopped

1. In a large bowl beat butter and peanut butter with a mixer on medium 30 seconds. Add both sugars and baking powder; beat until combined, scraping bowl as needed. Beat in egg, egg yolks, and vanilla. Beat in flour.
2. Preheat oven to 350°F. Grease a cookie sheet or line with parchment paper. For filling, in a small bowl combine jam and dried cherries.
3. On a lightly floured surface, roll one portion of dough at a time to ⅛-inch thickness. Using a 2½-inch scalloped round cookie cutter, cut out dough, rerolling scraps as needed.
4. Spoon 1 tsp. filling onto each cookie center. Fold dough edges in three places to form a triangular "hat," leaving opening in center. Place 2 inches apart on prepared cookie sheet.
5. Bake 8 to 9 minutes or until edges are light brown. Cool on cookie sheet 2 minutes. Transfer to a wire rack to cool. Makes 50 servings.
*Tip Do not use refrigerated natural peanut butter, which separates.
PER SERVING *139 cal., 7 g fat (3 g sat. fat), 21 mg chol., 71 mg sodium, 18 g carb., 1 g fiber, 2 g pro.*

SUGAR COOKIES

PREP 40 minutes
CHILL 30 minutes
BAKE 7 minutes per batch at 375°F

1   cup butter, softened
1¼ cups sugar
1½ tsp. baking powder
½   tsp. salt
2   eggs
2   tsp. vanilla
3   cups all-purpose flour
1   recipe Royal Icing (optional)

1. In a large bowl beat butter with a mixer on medium 30 seconds. Add sugar, baking powder, and salt and beat until combined, scraping bowl as needed. Beat in eggs and vanilla. Beat in flour. Divide dough in half. Cover and chill 30 minutes or until dough is easy to handle.
2. Preheat oven to 375°F. On a lightly floured surface, roll one portion of dough at a time until ⅛- to ¼-inch thick. Using 2½-inch cookie cutters, cut dough into desired shapes. Place 1 inch apart on an ungreased cookie sheet.
3. Bake 7 minutes or until edges are firm and bottoms are very light brown. Remove; cool on a wire rack. If desired, decorate with Royal Icing. Makes 52 servings.
PER SERVING *80 cal., 4 g fat (2 g sat. fat), 17 mg chol., 63 mg sodium, 10 g carb., 0 g fiber, 1 g pro.*
Royal Icing In a large bowl stir together one 16-oz. pkg. powdered sugar (4 cups), 3 Tbsp. meringue powder, and ½ tsp. cream of tartar. Add ½ cup warm water and 1 tsp. vanilla. Beat on low until combined; beat on high 7 to 10 minutes or until icing is very stiff. Use immediately or cover bowl with a damp paper towel; cover with plastic wrap. Chill up to 48 hours before using.

SUGAR
COOKIES

GINGER LINZER
COOKIES

GINGER LINZER COOKIES

PREP 40 minutes
CHILL 1 hour
BAKE 6 minutes per batch at 375°F

⅓   cup butter, softened
⅓   cup shortening
½   cup granulated sugar
1½ tsp. baking powder
¾   tsp. ground ginger
¼   tsp. salt
¼   tsp. ground cinnamon
¼   tsp. ground cloves
1   egg
⅓   cup molasses
1   Tbsp. cider vinegar
½   tsp. lemon zest
½   tsp. vanilla
2   cups all-purpose flour
    Powdered sugar
⅓   to ½ cup fig jam or cookie butter

1. In a large bowl beat butter and shortening with a mixer on medium 30 seconds. Add the next six ingredients (through cloves) and beat until combined, scraping bowl as needed. Beat in egg, molasses, vinegar, lemon zest, and vanilla. Beat in flour. Divide dough in half. Cover and chill 1 hour or until dough is easy to handle.
2. Preheat oven to 375°F. On a lightly floured surface, roll one portion of dough at a time to ⅛-inch thickness. Using 2½-inch cookie cutters, cut dough into desired shapes. (Reroll scraps as needed.) Place 1 inch apart on an ungreased cookie sheet. Using ¾-inch cookie cutters, cut out centers from half the cookies.
3. Bake 6 to 8 minutes or until edges are light brown. Remove; cool on a wire rack.
4. Sift powdered sugar over cookies with cutout centers. Spread bottoms of whole cookies with about 1 tsp. jam. Top with powdered sugar-dusted cookies, bottom sides down. Serve within 2 hours. Makes 20 servings.
To Store Layer unfilled cookies between waxed paper in an airtight container. Store at room temperature up to 3 days or freeze up to 3 months. To serve, thaw cookies if frozen. Fill cookies as directed.
PER SERVING *154 cal., 7 g fat (3 g sat. fat), 17 mg chol., 96 mg sodium, 22 g carb., 0 g fiber, 2 g pro.*

COCOA AND BROWN BUTTER SHORTBREAD BITES

PREP 20 minutes
CHILL 2 hours
BAKE 20 minutes at 325°F

1   cup butter, cut up
2   cups flour
¾   cup granulated sugar
6   Tbsp. unsweetened cocoa powder
4   oz. bittersweet chocolate, chopped
2   tsp. vegetable shortening

1. In a medium light-color* saucepan or skillet heat butter over medium-low until melted. Cook, stirring constantly, until butter is golden brown and brown specks form in bottom of pan. Transfer to a medium bowl. Refrigerate 30 minutes or until almost firm. (If butter is too firm, let stand at room temperature 15 to 20 minutes.) Meanwhile, line two baking sheets with parchment paper.
2. In a small bowl stir together flour, sugar, and cocoa. Beat butter with a mixer on medium 1 to 2 minutes or until creamy. Stir in flour mixture until dough begins to come together. Press dough into an 8-inch square on a prepared baking sheet.**
3. With a sharp knife score top of dough ¼ inch deep into 36 pieces. Cover with plastic wrap. Chill 2 to 24 hours.
4. Preheat oven to 325°F. Cut dough along scored lines; place 1 inch apart on prepared baking sheets. Bake 20 minutes or until firm. Cool completely on baking sheets.
5. In a small bowl microwave chocolate and shortening on medium 1 minute; stir. Continue heating and stirring chocolate at 10- to 15-second intervals until smooth. Dip cookies halfway in chocolate, scraping excess chocolate from bottoms on bowl rim. Let cookies stand on a parchment-lined baking sheet until set. Makes 36 servings.
*Tip Use a light-color skillet or saucepan (such as stainless steel) to easily see browned butter specks and help avoid burning the butter.
**Tip Or line an 8×8-inch baking pan with an 8-inch wide strip of parchment paper, overlapping two sides about 1 inch. Press dough into prepared pan. Using the paper, lift dough out of pan. Continue with Step 3.
PER SERVING *107 cal., 7 g fat (4 g sat. fat), 14 mg chol., 41 mg sodium, 12 g carb., 1 g fiber, 1 g pro.*

COCOA AND BROWN BUTTER SHORTBREAD BITES

TINY APPLE
CRISP TASSIES

5 WAYS WITH
CANDY BARK

TINY APPLE CRISP TASSIES

PREP 35 minutes
BAKE 15 minutes at 350°F
COOL 10 minutes

        Nonstick cooking spray
2   cups peeled and chopped apples,
        such as Braeburn, Jonagold, Pink
        Lady, or McIntosh
2   Tbsp. apple juice
1   Tbsp. granulated sugar
½   tsp. apple pie spice or ground
        cinnamon
¾   cup all-purpose flour
¾   cup regular rolled oats
½   cup packed brown sugar
¾   cup butter, cut up
3   Tbsp. finely chopped pecans,
        toasted (tip, page 22)
        Whipped cream or vanilla ice
        cream (optional)

1. Preheat oven to 350°F. Coat twenty-four 1¾-inch muffin cups with cooking spray.
2. For filling, in a medium saucepan combine chopped apples, apple juice, granulated sugar, and ¼ tsp. of the apple pie spice. Bring to boiling; reduce heat. Simmer 5 to 8 minutes or until apples are tender.
3. In a food processor combine flour, half the oats, the brown sugar, and remaining ¼ tsp. apple pie spice. Cover and process until combined. Add butter; cover and process until coarse crumbs form. Stir in remaining oats and the pecans.
4. Spoon 1 Tbsp. oat mixture into prepared muffin cups, pressing onto bottoms and up sides of cups. Spoon 2 tsp. filling into each crust-lined cup. Sprinkle with remaining oat mixture.
5. Bake 15 to 20 minutes or until golden. Cool in muffin pan(s) 10 minutes. Remove

tassies from pan(s). Serve warm. If desired, top with whipped cream. Makes 24 servings.
PER SERVING *106 cal., 7 g fat (4 g sat. fat), 15 mg chol., 47 mg sodium, 11 g carb., 1 g fiber, 1 g pro.*

5 WAYS WITH CANDY BARK

PREP 20 minutes
CHILL 30 minutes

6   oz. chocolate- or vanilla-flavor
        candy coating (almond bark),
        chopped
6   oz. milk, semisweet, or dark
        chocolate, chopped, or white
        baking chips
1   Tbsp. shortening
1   cup chopped assorted candy bars
½   cup chopped toasted pecans,
        walnuts, or almonds

1. Line a large baking sheet with heavy foil; grease foil. In a large bowl combine candy coating, chocolate, and shortening. Microwave 1½ to 2 minutes or until chocolate is melted, stirring every 30 seconds.

2. Pour melted candy onto prepared baking sheet and spread ¼ inch thick. Sprinkle with candy bars and nuts. Chill 30 minutes or until firm. Break candy into pieces. Makes 36 servings.
PER SERVING *75 cal., 5 g fat (3 g sat. fat), 3 mg chol., 10 mg sodium, 8 g carb., 1 g fiber, 1 g pro*

Salted Caramel Prepare and spread chocolate mixture as directed. In a medium bowl microwave half a 14-oz. pkg. vanilla caramels, unwrapped, and 1 Tbsp. milk 1 to 2 minutes or until melted, stirring every 30 seconds. Drizzle melted candy with melted caramels. Sprinkle with ¾ cup chopped toasted almonds and ¼ tsp. sea salt. Chill as directed.

S'mores Bark Using vanilla coating, prepare and spread melted candy as directed. Sprinkle with candy bars. Top with tiny marshmallows and coarsely crushed graham crackers. Chill as directed.

Sugar Cookie Bark Using vanilla coating, prepare and spread melted candy as directed. Sprinkle with crushed sugar cookies and red, white, and green sprinkles or jimmies. Chill as directed.

Mint Chocolate Line baking sheet with foil; grease foil. Arrange 9 chocolate wafer cookies on prepared cookie sheet. Using vanilla coating, melt half the candy with 3 oz. milk chocolate chips and ½ Tbsp. shortening. Melt remaining coating with 3 oz. green mint-flavor baking chips. Drop alternating spoonfuls of chocolate and mint mixtures onto cookies. Using a narrow spatula, swirl mixtures. Sprinkle with chopped layered chocolate-mint candies. Chill as directed.

PEANUT BUTTER AND MARSHMALLOW FUDGE

PREP 20 minutes
CHILL 2 hours

1   lb. white baking chocolate, chopped
¾   cup creamy peanut butter
1   14-oz. can sweetened condensed milk
1   Tbsp. vanilla
1   tsp. kosher salt
3   cups tiny marshmallows
2   cups salted, roasted peanuts, chopped
    Sea salt flakes
    Turbinado sugar

1. Grease a 9-inch square baking pan. Line with parchment paper, extending edges over pan. Grease paper.
2. Place white chocolate and peanut butter in a large heatproof bowl. Set bowl over a pan of simmering water. (Water should not touch bottom of bowl.) Stir occasionally until melted and smooth. Stir in sweetened condensed milk, vanilla, and kosher salt until combined. Remove from heat.
3. Stir in marshmallows and peanuts. Transfer to prepared pan. Cover with plastic wrap; flatten fudge evenly. Remove plastic wrap. Sprinkle with sea salt and sugar.
4. Chill, covered, 2 hours or until firm. Cut into 1-inch pieces. Makes 81 servings.
To Store Layer fudge between waxed paper in an airtight container. Store in refrigerator up to 1 week or freeze up to 2 months.
PER SERVING *88 cal., 5 g fat (2 g sat. fat), 3 mg chol., 65 mg sodium, 9 g carb., 0 g fiber, 2 g pro.*

PEANUT BUTTER AND MARSHMALLOW FUDGE

MEYER LEMON BLONDIES

PREP 30 minutes
BAKE 30 minutes at 350°F

Nonstick cooking spray
2 cups sugar
¾ cup butter
2 cups all-purpose flour
1 tsp. baking powder
¼ tsp. salt
2 eggs, lightly beaten
1 Tbsp. Meyer lemon zest or lemon zest
1 recipe Meyer Lemon Icing

1. Preheat oven to 350°F. Line a 9-inch square baking pan with foil, extending foil over edges of pan. Coat foil with cooking spray.

2. In a large saucepan cook and stir sugar and butter over medium 6 minutes or until melted and nearly smooth. Cool 10 minutes.

3. Meanwhile, in a medium bowl stir together flour, baking powder, and salt.

4. Stir eggs and lemon zest into butter mixture. Stir in flour mixture. Spread in prepared pan. Bake 30 minutes. Cool in pan on a wire rack. Use foil to lift uncut bars out of pan. Drizzle with Meyer Lemon Icing. Cut into bars. Makes 36 servings.

Meyer Lemon Icing In a small bowl stir together 1 cup powdered sugar, ¼ tsp. Meyer lemon zest or lemon zest, and 1 Tbsp. Meyer lemon juice or lemon juice until smooth. If needed, stir in additional lemon juice, 1 tsp. at a time, to make thick drizzling consistency.

PER SERVING *120 cal., 4 g fat (3 g sat. fat), 21 mg chol., 64 mg sodium, 20 g carb., 0 g fiber, 1 g pro.*

MEYER LEMON BLONDIES

CARAMEL-COCONUT COOKIE BARS

PREP 30 minutes
BAKE 20 minutes at 350°F
CHILL 1 hour

Nonstick cooking spray
1½ cups all-purpose flour
1 Tbsp. cornstarch
½ tsp. baking powder
½ tsp. salt
½ cup butter, softened
¼ cup granulated sugar
¼ cup packed brown sugar
1 egg yolk
1 tsp. vanilla
1 13.4-oz. can dulce de leche
3 Tbsp. milk
1 14-oz. pkg. sweetened flaked coconut
1 12-oz. pkg. semisweet chocolate chips (2 cups)

1. Preheat oven to 350°F. Line a 13×9-inch baking pan with foil, extending foil over edges of pan. Coat foil with cooking spray.
2. For crust, in a small bowl stir together flour, cornstarch, baking powder, and salt. In a large bowl beat butter with a mixer on medium 30 seconds. Add both sugars and beat on medium to high until light and fluffy. Beat in egg yolk and vanilla. Beat in flour mixture (mixture will be crumbly). Press onto bottom of prepared pan. Bake 10 to 12 minutes or until edges are light brown.
3. Meanwhile, in a large bowl combine dulce de leche and milk. Stir in coconut.
4. Sprinkle 1½ cups of the chocolate chips over hot crust; let stand 5 minutes. Spread chocolate over crust. Carefully spread coconut mixture over chocolate layer. Bake 10 minutes more. Cool in pan on a wire rack.
5. In a small bowl microwave remaining ½ cup chocolate chips 30 to 45 seconds or until melted and smooth, stirring once. Drizzle over bars. Cover and chill 1 hour or until set. Use foil to lift uncut bars out of pan. Cut into bars. Makes 24 servings.
PER SERVING *278 cal., 14 g fat (10 g sat. fat), 23 mg chol., 160 mg sodium, 37 g carb., 3 g fiber, 3 g pro.*

CARAMEL-COCONUT COOKIE BARS

CASHEW
CARMELITA BARS

CASHEW CARMELITA BARS

PREP 20 minutes
BAKE 28 minutes at 350°F
COOL 10 minutes

1¼ cups all-purpose flour
1¼ cups rolled oats
¾ cup packed brown sugar
¾ cup butter, melted
¾ tsp. baking soda
¼ tsp. salt
1 13.4-oz. can dulce de leche
1 cup chopped dry-roasted cashews
1 cup semisweet chocolate chips

1. Preheat oven to 350°F. Line an 8-inch square baking pan with foil, extending foil over edges of pan. Lightly grease foil.
2. For crust, in a large bowl stir together the first six ingredients (through salt). Reserve 1 cup of the oat mixture for topping. Press remaining mixture into prepared pan. Bake 10 to 12 minutes or until light brown. Cool on a wire rack 10 minutes.
3. Spread crust with dulce de leche. Sprinkle with cashews, chocolate chips, and reserved oat mixture; press lightly. Bake 18 to 22 minutes or until golden.
4. While warm, use a knife or thin spatula to loosen uncut bars from sides of pan. Cool in pan on a wire rack. Use foil to lift uncut bars out of pan. Cut into bars. Makes 36 servings.
PER SERVING *156 cal., 8 g fat (4 g sat. fat), 13 mg chol., 89 mg sodium, 20 g carb., 1 g fiber, 2 g pro.*

MALTED MILLIONAIRE'S SHORTBREAD

PREP 30 minutes
BAKE 18 minutes at 350°F
CHILL 1 hour 30 minutes
STAND 35 minutes

1 cup butter, softened
⅔ cup packed brown sugar
⅓ cup granulated sugar
1 egg yolk
2 tsp. vanilla
½ tsp. salt
½ cup malted milk powder
1¾ cups all-purpose flour
⅓ cup butter, cut up
1 14-oz. can sweetened condensed milk

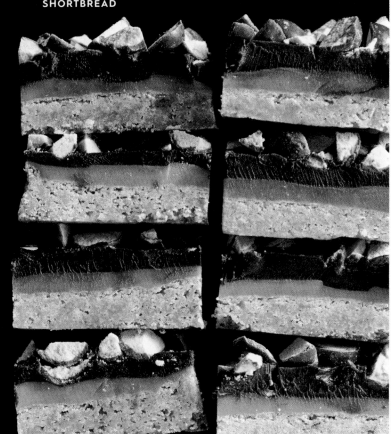

MALTED MILLIONAIRE'S SHORTBREAD

½ cup heavy cream
1 12-oz. pkg. semisweet chocolate chips
Coarsely chopped malted milk balls

1. Preheat oven to 350°F. Line a 13×9-inch baking pan with parchment paper, extending paper over edges of pan.
2. For crust, in a large bowl beat 1 cup butter with a mixer on medium 30 seconds. Add ⅓ cup of the brown sugar and granulated sugar; beat 1 to 2 minutes or until light and fluffy. Beat in egg yolk, 1 tsp. of the vanilla, and the salt until combined. Beat in malted milk powder. Gradually beat in flour just until combined (mixture will be crumbly). Press into prepared pan.
3. Bake 18 to 22 minutes or until edges are golden and center is set. Cool in pan on a wire rack.
4. Meanwhile, for caramel layer, in a medium saucepan stir ⅓ cup butter and remaining ⅓ cup brown sugar over medium until melted. Stir in sweetened condensed milk. Bring to boiling over medium-high; reduce heat. Simmer 15 minutes or until golden, stirring constantly. Remove from heat. Stir in remaining 1 tsp. vanilla. Spread caramel over crust. Cover and chill 1 hour or until set.
5. For chocolate layer, in a small saucepan bring cream just to simmering over medium heat. Remove from heat. Add chocolate chips (do not stir). Let stand 5 minutes. Stir until smooth. Spread over caramel layer. Sprinkle with chopped malted milk balls. Cover and chill 30 minutes or until set.
6. Use edges of parchment paper to lift uncut bars out of pan. Cut into bars. Let stand at room temperature at least 30 minutes before serving. Makes 24 servings.
PER SERVING *314 cal., 18 g fat (11 g sat. fat), 46 mg chol., 171 mg sodium, 37 g carb., 1 g fiber, 3 g pro.*

EGGNOG DREAM BARS

EGGNOG DREAM BARS

PREP 20 minutes
FREEZE 20 minutes
BAKE 35 minutes at 350°F

Nonstick cooking spray
10 Tbsp. unsalted butter, melted and slightly cooled
5 Tbsp. rum (optional)
4 tsp. ground cinnamon
2 cups finely crushed graham cracker crumbs (12 rectangle crackers)
2 cups shredded sweetened coconut
1 14-oz. can sweetened condensed milk
2 tsp. vanilla
1 tsp. freshly grated nutmeg or ½ teaspoon ground nutmeg
⅛ tsp. ground cloves
1¼ cups chopped walnuts, toasted (tip, page 22)
1 cup bittersweet chocolate chips
½ cup milk chocolate chips
½ cup white baking chips

1. Preheat oven to 350°F. Line a 13×9-inch baking pan with foil, extending foil over edges of pan. Coat with nonstick cooking spray.
2. For crust, in a large bowl combine butter, 2 Tbsp. rum (if using), and 2 tsp. cinnamon. Stir in cracker crumbs and 1 cup coconut to combine. Transfer to prepared pan. Press firmly and evenly into bottom of pan. Freeze 20 minutes.
3. Bake crust 10 minutes or until lightly browned. Place pan on a wire rack.
4. For drizzle, in a medium bowl whisk together sweetened condensed milk, 3 Tbsp. rum (if using), vanilla, remaining 2 tsp. cinnamon, nutmeg, and cloves. Set aside. Sprinkle walnuts, and bittersweet, milk, white chocolate baking chips over crust. Top with remaining 1 cup coconut. Drizzle sweetened condensed milk mixture.
5. Bake 25 to 30 minutes or until filling is set and lightly browned, rotating pan once halfway through baking. Cool on a wire rack. Use foil to lift uncut bars out of pan. Cut into bars. Makes 24 servings.
PER SERVING *302 cal., 19 g fat (11 g sat. fat), 20 mg chol., 103 mg sodium, 31 g carb., 2 g fiber, 4 g pro.*

IRISH CREAM PUDDING BARS

IRISH CREAM PUDDING BARS

PREP 35 minutes
CHILL 3 hours

1¼ cups chocolate sandwich cookie baking crumbs, chocolate graham cracker crumbs, or crushed chocolate wafer cookies
¼ cup granulated sugar
¼ cup finely chopped pecans or walnuts
⅓ cup butter, melted
¼ cup butter, softened
¼ cup vanilla instant pudding and pie filling mix
2 Tbsp. heavy cream
2 Tbsp. Irish cream liqueur or almond milk liqueur
1½ cups powdered sugar
6 oz. bittersweet chocolate, coarsely chopped
¼ cup butter
2 oz. white baking chocolate, melted (optional)

1. Line a 9-inch square baking pan with foil, extending foil over edges of pan. For crust, in a small bowl stir together cookie crumbs, granulated sugar, and nuts. Stir in melted butter until combined. Press into prepared pan.
2. For filling, in a large bowl combine softened butter, pudding mix, cream, and liqueur. Beat with a mixer on medium until smooth. Gradually beat in powdered sugar. Beat on medium to high 2 to 3 minutes or until light and fluffy. Carefully spread filling over crust. Cover and chill 1 hour or until firm.
3. For topping, in a small saucepan stir bittersweet chocolate and ¼ cup butter over low heat until melted. Spread over filling. If desired, drizzle or spoon melted white chocolate over topping; swirl slightly with a toothpick to marble. Cover and chill 2 hours or until firm. Use foil to lift uncut bars out of pan. Cut into bars. Makes 25 servings.
PER SERVING *188 cal., 13 g fat (7 g sat. fat), 19 mg chol., 83 mg sodium, 20 g carb., 1 g fiber, 1 g pro.*

APPLE CINNAMON
BREAD, PAGE 127

Gifts of Gratitude

Show your appreciation for neighbors,
teachers, and holiday party guests with
gifts from your kitchen.

SHORTBREAD
BOURBON-VANILLA
COOKIE BUTTER,
PAGE 122

FRUIT AND
NUTS OATMEAL

FRUIT AND NUTS OATMEAL

PREP 35 minutes
BAKE 15 minutes at 350°F

2   cups regular rolled oats
½   cup coarsely chopped pecans, walnuts, or almonds
⅔   cup nonfat dry milk powder
¼   cup packed brown sugar
2   tsp. ground cinnamon, apple pie spice, or pumpkin pie spice
½   tsp. salt
⅓   cup toasted wheat germ or oat bran
½   cup snipped dried fruit, such as apricots, peaches, pitted dates, figs, and/or apples, or dried fruit, such as tart red cherries, raisins, golden raisins, blueberries, and/or cranberries
     Honey (optional)

1. Preheat oven to 350°F. Spread oats and nuts in a shallow baking pan. Bake 15 to 20 minutes or until oats are lightly browned, stirring twice. Cool in pan on a wire rack.
2. In a 1-qt. glass jar use a funnel or waxed or parchment paper rolled into a funnel to layer ingredients in the following order: half the oat mixture, dry milk powder, brown sugar, cinnamon, salt, wheat germ, dried fruit, and remaining oat mixture. Lightly tap jar on counter to settle each layer before adding the next.
3. Directions for Fruit and Nuts Oatmeal: Shake ingredients in jar to mix. For two servings, in a medium saucepan bring 1½ cups water and, if desired, 1 Tbsp. butter to boiling. Add ⅔ cup of jar contents; reduce heat. Simmer, uncovered, 10 to 12 minutes or until oatmeal reaches desired consistency (oatmeal will thicken slightly as it cools). Let stand 1 to 2 minutes before serving. If desired, drizzle oatmeal with honey. Makes 12 servings.
PER SERVING *118 cal., 4 g fat (0 g sat. fat), 1 mg chol., 103 mg sodium, 18 g carb., 2 g fiber, 4 g pro.*
As a Gift Tie a coordinating jingle bell in the center of a yarn pom-pom. Loop a length of ribbon, top with pom-pom, and hot glue trim in place. Attach directions for serving.

CHOCOLATE-CHERRY PANCAKE MIX

CHOCOLATE-CHERRY PANCAKE MIX

START TO FINISH 30 minutes

1⅔   cups all-purpose flour
¼   cup sugar
1   tsp. baking soda
¼   tsp. salt
⅓   cup unsweetened cocoa powder
½   cup miniature semisweet chocolate pieces, snipped dried cherries, or chopped toasted walnuts (optional)
¼   cup snipped dried cherries
1   recipe Cinnamon Cider Syrup or purchased pancake syrup (optional)

1. In a small bowl stir together flour, sugar, baking soda, and salt. Transfer to a plastic bag; tie closed with a ribbon. Package the cocoa powder, chocolate pieces (if using), and dried cherries each in separate bags tie with ribbons.
2. Directions for Chocolate-Cherry Pancakes: In a large bowl combine 1 lightly beaten egg, 2¼ cups buttermilk, 3 Tbsp. vegetable oil, and 1 tsp. vanilla. Add pancake mix. Stir just until moistened (batter should be slightly lumpy). For each pancake, pour about ¼ cup batter onto a hot, lightly greased griddle or heavy skillet. Cook over medium heat 2 to 3 minutes on each side or until undersides are golden brown, surfaces are bubbly, and edges are slightly dry. Serve warm. Makes 18 pancakes.
PER SERVING *119 cal., 6 g fat (2 g sat. fat), 23 mg chol., 142 mg sodium, 14 g carb., 1 g fiber, 3 g pro.*
As a Gift Nestle bags in a mixing bowl lined with a holiday towel and tissue paper. Add a colorful spatula and, if desired, Cinnamon Cider Syrup. Attach directions for Chocolate-Cherry Pancakes.

Cinnamon Cider Syrup In a 5- to 6-qt. Dutch oven bring 8 cups apple cider or apple juice to boiling. Boil gently, uncovered, 1¾ hours or until reduced to 1½ cups, stirring occasionally. Remove from heat; cool to room temperature. In a small saucepan stir together ¼ cup packed brown sugar, 2 tsp. cornstarch, and ½ tsp. ground cinnamon. Add reduced cider, 2 Tbsp. butter, and ½ tsp. vanilla. Cook and stir over medium until thickened and bubbly. Cook and stir 2 minutes more. Remove saucepan from heat; cool. Transfer cooled syrup to a clean screw-top jar. Cover and refrigerate up to 3 months.

VANILLA EXTRACT

PREP 10 minutes
STAND 1 month

½ cup bourbon, vodka, brandy, or rum
2 vanilla beans, split lengthwise and cut into small pieces

1. In an 8-oz. glass jar combine liquor and vanilla bean pieces (make sure the vanilla pieces are submerged in the liquor). Cover and let stand in a cool, dark place at least 1 month, shaking jar once a week to help distribute flavor. (Taste extract after 1 month; let stand longer for stronger flavor.)

2. To use, strain the extract through a fine-mesh sieve lined with two layers of 100%-cotton cheesecloth to remove vanilla bean pieces.

3. Transfer extract to a bottle; seal. Store in a cool, dark place up to 1 year. Makes ½ cup.

PER SERVING *0 cal., 0 g fat, 0 mg chol., 0 mg sodium, 0 g carb., 0 g fiber, 0 g pro.*

Tip If you do not strain Vanilla Extract, replenish it by adding more liquor. However, once the vanilla is no longer adds flavor, strain the extract and add fresh pieces of vanilla beans.

Coffee Extract Prepare as directed, using vodka, brandy, or rum for the liquor. Substitute ¼ cup coffee beans, finely crushed, for vanilla beans. Use for baking and to flavor frosting and beverages.

As a Gift Long-neck bottles leave room for decoration without getting in the way of pouring. For color, hot-glue wide ribbon around the bottle neck. Wire together a small arrangement of pinecones, berries, and faux leaves, then tie to the bottle with narrow ribbon.

COLD BREW COFFEE

PREP 5 minutes
STAND 12 hours

6 cups cold water
1½ cups coarsely ground coffee

1. In a 2-qt. pitcher or glass jar stir the water into ground coffee. Cover with plastic wrap and let stand at room temperature 12 to 24 hours.

2. Line a fine-mesh sieve with 100%-cotton cheesecloth or a coffee filter; pour coffee through sieve into a large bowl or another 2-qt. container. Store coffee in refrigerator up to 2 weeks. Makes 6 servings.

PER SERVING *2 cal., 0 g fat, 0 mg chol., 4 mg sodium, 0 g carb., 0 g fiber, 0 g pro.*

As a Gift Paint a wooden snowflake red using cross-hatch brush strokes; let dry. Print a small circle with "Baby It's Cold Outside!" to fit center of snowflake; cut out and adhere using a glue stick. Wrap a silver chenille stem around a small round object to shape to fit around printed circle. Trim chenille stem and hot-glue it in place. Drill a hole in snowflake, thread with chenille stem, and attach to a bold polka-dot bow.

VANILLA
EXTRACT

Baby It's Cold Outside!

COLD BREW COFFEE

SHORTBREAD BOURBON-VANILLA COOKIE BUTTER

PREP 10 minutes
STAND 15 minutes

½ cup milk
1 Tbsp. sugar
1 Tbsp. bourbon (optional)
1 10-oz. pkg. shortbread cookies, coarsely crushed
1 Tbsp. vanilla bean paste

1. In a medium saucepan heat and stir the first three ingredients (through bourbon) over medium heat until milk is warm and sugar is dissolved. Stir in crushed cookies; let stand 15 minutes.
2. Transfer mixture to a food processor or blender. Add vanilla bean paste. Cover and process or blend until smooth. Store in an airtight container in the refrigerator up to 2 weeks.
3. To serve cookie butter, scoop onto hot waffles, cobblers, or sautéed apple slices. Layer between graham crackers for s'mores. Makes 24 servings.
PER SERVING *65 cal., 3 g fat (1 g sat. fat), 0 mg chol., 66 mg sodium, 9 g carb., 0 g fiber, 1 g pro.*
As A Gift Remove lid insert and cut burlap to fit. Center clear double-sided tape on lid insert to secure burlap. Hot-glue a small cluster of mini pinecones, faux berries, and a ribbon bow to center. Cut a burlap strip to fit jar. Remove a thread or two along each long edge to fray. Pull and remove three or four threads from the center of the burlap piece. Weave ¼-inch-wide grosgrain ribbon through center of burlap, over three threads, under three threads to weave ribbon through burlap. Place around jar and knot ribbon ends.

DECADENT HOT CHOCOLATE MIX

START TO FINISH 20 minutes

1 cup sugar
1 cup unsweetened cocoa powder
2 cups nonfat dry milk powder
1½ cups semisweet chocolate pieces
1 cup crushed soft peppermint sticks

1. In three 1-pint plastic bags, use a funnel or waxed or parchment paper rolled into a funnel to layer ingredients equally in the following order: sugar, cocoa powder, milk powder, semisweet chocolate pieces, and crushed peppermint sticks. (Use a funnel or a piece of waxed or parchment paper that has been rolled into a funnel when layering ingredients.)
2. Directions for Decadent Hot Chocolate: In a large saucepan combine contents of bag with 1⅔ cups water. Heat and stir over medium heat until hot and chocolate pieces have melted. Pour into four mugs. If desired, serve with marshmallows. Makes 12 servings.
PER SERVING *282 cal., 7 g fat (4 g sat. fat), 2 mg chol., 66 mg sodium, 54 g carb., 3 g fiber, 6 g pro.*
As a Gift Wrap a clean can (with no sharp edges) with print cardstock using hot-glue to secure. Hot-glue trim to the rim and add a ribbon bow and button. Place hot chocolate mix into a clear cellophane bag, close with a twist tie, and place in the can. Attach directions for Decadent Hot Chocolate.

SHORTBREAD BOURBON-VANILLA COOKIE BUTTER

CRANBERRY-
ORANGE
CARAMEL CORN

CRANBERRY-ORANGE CARAMEL CORN

PREP 25 minutes
BAKE 30 minutes at 275°F

12 cups popped popcorn
1 cup dried cranberries
½ cup whole almonds
½ cup butter
½ cup packed brown sugar
¼ cup light-color corn syrup
2 Tbsp. orange juice
2 tsp. vanilla
½ tsp. baking soda

1. Preheat oven to 275°F. In an extra-large bowl combine popped popcorn, dried cranberries, and almonds.
2. In a 2-qt. saucepan stir butter, brown sugar, and corn syrup over medium heat until butter is melted. Stir in orange juice. Bring to boiling over medium heat. Boil at a moderate, steady rate 2 minutes. Remove from heat. Stir in vanilla and baking soda (mixture will foam up).
3. Pour syrup over popcorn mixture; stir to coat well. Transfer to a 15×10-inch baking pan or shallow roasting pan. Bake 30 minutes, stirring twice. Transfer caramel corn to a large sheet of greased heavy foil to cool. Store caramel corn in covered container. Makes 10 servings.
PER SERVING *130 cal., 7 g fat (3 g sat. fat), 12 mg chol., 68 mg sodium, 17 g carb., 1 g fiber, 10 g sugars, 1 g pro.*
As a Gift Wrap a cardboard cone, available at crafts stores, with decorative paper, trim to fit, and adhere with a glue stick. Hot-glue tinsel garland around the opening. If desired, glue a row of buttons along one side. Tuck a triangular icing bag into the cone, fill with popcorn mix, then tie closed with ribbon.

ELFIN SHORTBREAD BITES

ELFIN SHORTBREAD BITES

PREP 20 minutes
BAKE 12 minutes at 325°F

1¼ cups all-purpose flour
3 Tbsp. sugar
½ cup butter
2 Tbsp. colored sprinkles

1. Preheat oven to 325°F. In a medium bowl stir together flour and sugar. Using a pastry blender, cut in butter until mixture resembles fine crumbs and starts to cling. Stir in colored sprinkles. Form dough into a ball and knead until smooth.
2. On an ungreased cookie sheet roll or pat dough into an 8×5-inch rectangle. Cut into ½-inch squares. Separate squares on cookie sheet.

3. Bake 12 to 14 minutes or until bottoms just start to brown. Transfer to a wire rack covered with waxed paper to cool. Makes 36 servings.
PER SERVING *12 cal., 1 fat (0 g sat. fat), 2 mg chol., 7 mg sodium, 1 g carb., 0 g fiber, 0 g pro.*
As a Gift Use tissue paper rolls or trimmed paper towel or wrapping paper tubes for cylinders. Place a clear cellophane treat bag into a tube then fill with bites; close with a twist tie. Wrap the tube with gift wrap, allowing 3 extra inches on each end; tape seam in center. Pinch paper at tube ends; tie with ribbon. Add a holiday sticker to the center of each cracker.

FRESH
CRANBERRY
SCONES

FRESH CRANBERRY SCONES

PREP 20 minutes
BAKE 20 minutes at 375°F

2¼ cups all-purpose flour
2 Tbsp. granulated sugar
1 Tbsp. baking powder
¼ tsp. salt
1½ cups fresh cranberries, finely
    chopped
2 Tbsp. honey
1 cup heavy cream
1 egg, lightly beaten
1 Tbsp. water
    Coarse sugar

1. Preheat oven to 375°F. In a bowl stir together flour, 2 Tbsp. granulated sugar, baking powder, and salt. Make a well in center of flour mixture; set aside.
2. In another bowl stir together cranberries and honey; stir in cream. Add cranberry mixture to flour mixture all at once. Using a fork, stir just until moistened.
3. Turn dough out onto a lightly floured surface. Knead dough by folding and gently pressing 10 to 12 strokes or until nearly smooth. Pat or lightly roll dough into an 8-inch square. Cut into nine squares. Place squares about 1 inch apart on an ungreased baking sheet. In a bowl stir together the egg and water. Lightly brush wedges with egg mixture and sprinkle with coarse sugar.
4. Bake 20 to 25 minutes or until tops are golden brown. Remove scones from baking sheet; cool completely. Makes 9 servings.
PER SERVING *300 cal., 12 fat (7 g sat. fat), 68 mg chol., 184 mg sodium, 42 g carb., 20 g fiber, 6 g pro.*
As a Gift Place a food-safe plastic bag into a large mug then fill with scones. Use a wire tie to close bag. Thread narrow ribbon through a medium-size jingle bell and tie around bag top. Tuck in a sprig of artificial holly and berries to complete the wrap.
Fresh Cranberry-Chocolate Scones
Prepare as above, stirring ⅔ cup (3 oz.) coarsely chopped bittersweet chocolate into cranberry mixture.
Fresh Cranberry-Pecan Scones
Prepare as above, stirring ⅔ cup coarsely chopped toasted pecans into cranberry mixture.

APPLE CINNAMON BREAD

PREP 35 minutes
BAKE 50 minutes at 350°F
COOL 10 minutes

3 eggs, lightly beaten
½ cup vegetable oil
½ cup applesauce
2 cups sugar
2 large firm, tart apples, peeled,
    cored and shredded
2 tsp. vanilla
3 cups all-purpose flour
1 Tbsp. ground cinnamon
1 tsp. salt
1 tsp. baking power
1 tsp. baking soda
1 cup chopped pecans

1. Preheat oven to 350°F. Grease bottoms and ½ inch up sides of two 8×4×2-inch foil pans; lightly flour pans.
2. In a bowl combine eggs, oil, applesauce, and sugar; beat with a whisk or rotary beater. Stir in apple and vanilla. In another bowl combine flour, cinnamon, salt, baking powder, and baking soda; add to apple mixture. Stir to combine. Stir in nuts. Divide batter between prepared pans.
3. Bake 50 to 60 minutes or until a wooden toothpick inserted near centers comes out clean. Cool in pans on a wire rack 10 minutes. Remove from pans and cool completely. Wash and dry foil pans. Return cooled loaves to pans. Wrap tightly. Makes 32 servings
PER SERVING *257 cal., 10 g fat (1 g sat. fat), 32 mg chol., 209 mg sodium, 39 g carb., 2 g fiber, 2 g pro.*
As A Gift Dress up a wrapped loaf of bread with layered ribbons and cinnamon sticks tied to the top. Tuck in a few sprigs of fresh greenery.

APPLE CINNAMON BREAD

CHOCOLATE CAKE WITH
MALT TOPPING,
PAGE 142

New Year's Eve Party

Raise your glass and toast the coming year in style and good taste. Celebrate the occasion amid savory appetizers, indulgent desserts, and warming drinks.

SAVORY
CHARD PIE,
PAGE 137

129

SICILIAN POTATO CROQUETTES

PARMESAN-CRUSTED BRUSSELS SPROUTS

PREP 35 minutes
BAKE 15 minutes at 425°F

1   lb. Brussels sprouts, trimmed; halved if large
2   eggs
⅔   cup whole wheat panko bread crumbs
⅓   cup grated Parmesan cheese
½   tsp. garlic powder
½   tsp. salt
¼   tsp. black pepper
    Nonstick cooking spray
1   cup marinara sauce, warmed (optional)

1. Preheat oven to 425°F. Line a 15×10-inch baking pan with parchment paper.*
2. In a 4-qt. pot fitted with a steamer basket bring 2 inches of water to boiling. Add Brussels sprouts; cover and steam 5 to 7 minutes or until tender. Transfer to a paper-towel-lined plate and pat dry.
3. In a shallow dish lightly beat eggs. In another shallow dish stir together panko, Parmesan, garlic powder, salt, and pepper. Roll each sprout in egg to coat. Allow excess to drip off, then roll in panko mixture to coat. Place sprouts in prepared baking pan with space between pieces; lightly coat with cooking spray.
4. Bake 15 to 18 minutes or until golden brown and tender, turning once. If desired, serve with marinara sauce. Makes 8 servings.
***Tip** For large Brussels sprouts, you may need to use two large rimmed baking sheets to avoid crowding sprouts ins pans. Bake as directed in Step 4, switching the pan positions in oven halfway through.
PER SERVING *80 cal., 2 g fat (1 g sat. fat), 49 mg chol., 245 mg sodium, 10 g carb., 3 g fiber, 5 g pro.*

SICILIAN POTATO CROQUETTES

START TO FINISH 30 minutes

2   lb. boiling potatoes, such as russet or Yukon gold, peeled and quartered
1¾ tsp. salt
2   egg yolks
⅓   cup grated Romano cheese
¼   cup chopped green onions
¼   cup pine nuts
3   Tbsp. snipped fresh parsley
3   Tbsp. snipped fresh mint
¼   tsp. freshly ground black pepper
    Cooking oil for deep-fat frying
3   egg whites
½   cup all-purpose flour
1   cup plain fine dry bread crumbs

1. In a large saucepan cook potatoes in 1 tsp. of the salt in enough cold water to cover by 2 inches 12 to 15 minutes or until tender. Drain. Press potatoes through a potato ricer or food mill into a large bowl. Beat in remaining ¾ tsp. salt, egg yolks, cheese, green onions, pine nuts, parsley, mint, and pepper.
2. Preheat oven to 200°F. Line two shallow baking pans with foil. For each croquette, shape rounded tablespoons of potato mixture into 2-inch-long ovals. Place ovals in prepared pans.
3. In a large heavy saucepan or extra-large, deep skillet heat oil to 365°F over medium. Beat egg whites in bowl until frothy. Spread flour in a shallow dish and bread crumbs in second shallow dish. Dip potato pieces in flour, then egg whites, then coat in crumbs.
4. Fry potato pieces, five or six at a time, in hot oil 3 minutes or until golden. Use a slotted spoon to transfer croquettes to paper towels to drain. Keep croquettes warm in oven while frying remaining potato pieces. Serve warm. Makes 30 servings.
PER SERVING *75 cal., 4 g fat (1 g sat. fat), 15 mg chol., 153 mg sodium, 9 g carb., 0 g fiber, 2 g pro.*

PARMESAN-CRUSTED
BRUSSELS SPROUTS

ASIAN PORK
NACHOS WITH
WASABI CREAM

ASIAN PORK NACHOS WITH WASABI CREAM

PREP 15 minutes
BAKE 13 minutes at 425°F

12	6-inch extra-thin corn tortillas
	Nonstick cooking spray
6	oz. shredded cooked pork loin or chicken breast
1	Tbsp. reduced-sodium soy sauce
½	tsp. Chinese five-spice powder
2	Tbsp. light sour cream
2	Tbsp. plain fat-free Greek yogurt
2	tsp. water
½	tsp. wasabi paste
1	cup shredded reduced-fat cheddar cheese (4 oz.)
2	cups shredded cabbage with carrot (coleslaw mix)
¼	cup sliced green onions
¼	cup snipped fresh cilantro

1. Preheat oven to 425°F. Cut each tortilla into six wedges. Arrange wedges, one-third at a time, in a 15×10-inch baking pan; lightly coat with cooking spray. Bake 8 minutes or until light brown and crisp.
2. In a bowl combine shredded meat, soy sauce, and five-spice powder. For wasabi cream, in another bowl stir together sour cream, yogurt, water, and wasabi paste.
3. Spread baked tortilla wedges in baking pan. Top with meat mixture and sprinkle with cheese. Bake 5 minutes or until cheese is melted.
4. Top nachos with coleslaw mix, green onions, and cilantro. Drizzle with wasabi cream. Makes 4 servings.
PER SERVING *325 cal., 13 g fat (6 g sat. fat), 58 mg chol., 425 mg sodium, 29 g carb., 4 g fiber, 24 g pro.*

SPICY SUGARED ALMONDS

START TO FINISH 15 minutes

1	Tbsp. sugar
¼	tsp. ground cinnamon
¼	tsp. cayenne pepper
1½	cups sugar
½	cup plus 2 Tbsp. water
2½	cups whole almonds

1. Line a baking sheet with parchment paper. In a small bowl stir together Tbsp. sugar, cinnamon, and cayenne pepper; set aside.

SPICY SUGARED ALMONDS

2. In a 4-qt. saucepan combine 1½ cups sugar and water. Stir over medium-high until sugar is dissolved and mixture boils. Add almonds and stir constantly over medium-high until water evaporates and sugar starts to dry and turn gray. (Sugar mixture will foam then start to dry and look like sand. This step takes 5 to 6 minutes.) Continue stirring constantly 2 to 3 minutes or until sugar starts to melt and caramelize, coating almonds.

3. Sprinkle cinnamon mixture over almonds, stirring constantly. Immediately spread coated almonds on prepared baking sheet. Cool, then break apart. Store almonds in an airtight container up to 2 weeks. Makes 18 servings.
PER SERVING *183 cal., 10 g fat (1 g sat. fat), 0 mg chol., 1 mg sodium, 22 g carb., 3 g fiber, 4 g pro.*

**MOZZARELLA
CHEESE STICKS**

*Tip Or cut twelve 4×½-inch
cheese sticks from one 16-oz. block
mozzarella cheese.
Make Ahead Transfer frozen cheese
sticks to a freezer container; seal and
freeze up to 1 month. To serve, continue
with Steps 2 and 3.
PER SERVING 202 cal., 12 g fat
(4 g sat. fat), 46 mg chol., 533 mg
sodium, 15 g carb., 1 g fiber, 11 g pro.

HOT BROWN STROMBOLI

PREP 25 minutes
BAKE 40 minutes at 375°F
COOL 20 minutes

2   tsp. olive oil
1   Tbsp. cornmeal
1   lb. pkg. refrigerated or frozen
     pizza dough, thawed
3   Tbsp. Dijon mustard
8   oz. sliced deli cooked turkey
1½   cups shredded Gruyère cheese
     (6 oz.)
4   slices bacon, crisp-cooked and
     crumbled
1   cup chopped roma tomatoes
1   egg yolk
1   Tbsp. sesame seeds

1. Preheat oven to 375°F. Line a
15×10-inch baking pan with foil;
brush with 2 tsp. olive oil. Sprinkle
with cornmeal.
2. On a lightly floured surface, roll
dough to a 13×10-inch rectangle.
Transfer to prepared pan. Spread
dough with mustard then arrange
half the turkey on dough, leaving
½-inch borders. Sprinkle with half the
cheese. Top with bacon, tomatoes, and
remaining turkey and cheese.
3. Starting from a long side, roll up
dough around filling. Pinch seam and
ends to seal. Lightly beat egg yolk with
1 tsp. water. Brush dough with egg yolk
mixture; sprinkle with sesame seeds.
Using a sharp knife, cut shallow slits on
top to vent.
4. Bake 40 minutes or until golden
brown. Cool 20 minutes. Makes
8 servings.
PER SERVING 310 cal., 13 g fat
(5 g sat. fat), 63 mg chol., 787 mg
sodium, 28 g carb., 0 g fiber, 18 g pro.

MOZZARELLA CHEESE STICKS

PREP 20 minutes
FREEZE 1 hour
COOK 2 minutes

¾   cup all-purpose flour
½   tsp. salt
½   tsp. black pepper
2   eggs, lightly beaten
2   Tbsp. water
12   mozzarella cheese sticks (string
     cheese)*
1   cup seasoned fine dry bread
     crumbs
¼   cup vegetable oil
¾   cup marinara sauce, warmed

1. In a shallow dish stir together flour,
salt, and pepper. In another shallow
dish combine eggs and water. Dip
cheese sticks in egg mixture, then coat
with flour mixture. Dip again in egg
mixture, then coat with bread crumbs.
Place on a baking sheet. Freeze 1 hour
or until firm.**
2. To serve, in a large skillet heat oil
over medium. Add half the frozen
cheese sticks; cook 2 to 3 minutes
or until golden, turning occasionally.
Drain on paper towels. Repeat with
the remaining cheese sticks, adding
additional oil, if necessary.
3. In a saucepan heat marinara sauce
over medium heat. Serve cheese sticks
with warm marinara sauce. Makes
12 servings.

HOT BROWN
STROMBOLI

SAVORY
CHARD PIE

SAVORY CHARD PIE

PREP 20 minutes
BAKE 25 minutes at 375°F

1   14.1-oz. pkg. rolled refrigerated unbaked piecrust (2 piecrusts)
6   to 8 cups coarsely chopped chard with stems
4   oz. garlic-and-herb-flavor goat cheese
4   large dates, pitted and chopped
3   oz. thinly sliced ham, pancetta, or prosciutto
½   tsp. salt
½   tsp. black pepper

1. Preheat oven to 375°F. Let piecrusts stand according to package directions. In a large bowl gently massage chard 30 seconds (you should have about 3 cups).
2. Unroll piecrusts onto a lightly floured surface. Cut each crust in half. Roll or press each half with your hands until wide enough to cut around an 8-inch plate with a small knife. Transfer rounds to a baking sheet.
3. Layer chard, goat cheese, dates, and ham in center of each round, leaving 1½-inch borders. Lift and fold edge over filling, pleating as necessary, leaving center filling exposed. Sprinkle with salt and pepper. Bake 25 to 30 minutes or until golden. Makes 4 servings.
PER SERVING *601 cal., 37 g fat (16 g sat. fat), 42 mg chol., 1,119 mg sodium, 57 g carb., 2 g fiber, 13 g pro.*

AVOCADO FRIES

PREP 15 minutes
BAKE 10 minutes at 425°F

    Nonstick cooking spray
2   medium firm ripe avocados, halved, seeded, peeled, and cut into ½-inch wedges
    Salt and black pepper
⅓   cup all-purpose flour
2   eggs, lightly beaten
1   cup finely crushed tortilla chips* or panko bread crumbs
    Chili powder (optional)

1. Preheat oven to 425°F. Line a baking sheet with parchment paper or foil; coat with cooking spray. Sprinkle avocado wedges with salt and pepper.
2. Place flour in a shallow bowl. Place eggs in another shallow bowl.

AVOCADO FRIES

Place crushed tortilla chips in a third shallow bowl.
3. Dip seasoned avocado wedges in flour, turning to coat. Dip in eggs, turning to coat. Dip in crushed tortilla chips, pressing chips gently onto wedges as necessary to coat.
4. Arrange coated avocado wedges on prepared baking sheet. Lightly coat avocado wedges with cooking spray. If desired, sprinkle wedges with chili powder. Bake 10 to 12 minutes or until golden brown, turning once. Makes 4 servings.
***Tip** To crush tortilla chips, place them in a resealable plastic bag; seal bag. Roll a rolling pin over bag to finely crush chips.
PER SERVING *272 cal., 17 g fat (3 g sat. fat), 93 mg chol., 261 mg sodium, 26 g carb., 6 g fiber, 7 g pro.*

ROASTED SWEET POTATO FRIES

PREP 10 minutes
ROAST 20 minutes at 450°F

2   lb. sweet potatoes, cut lengthwise into ½-inch strips
¼   cup olive oil
1   tsp. salt
½   tsp. black pepper
    Snipped fresh parsley (optional)

1. Preheat oven to 450°F. Line two shallow baking pans with foil. Place sweet potatoes in prepared pans. Drizzle with oil and sprinkle with salt and pepper; toss to coat.
2. Roast 15 minutes. Turn sweet potatoes. Roast 5 to 10 minutes more or until tender and light brown. If desired, sprinkle with parsley. Makes 6 servings.
Tip For extra flavor, toss sweet potatoes with 1 Tbsp. sugar and 1 tsp. each ground cumin and chili powder before roasting.
PER SERVING *174 cal., 9 g fat (1 g sat. fat), 0 mg chol., 448 mg sodium, 22 g carb., 4 g fiber, 2 g pro.*

SUN-DRIED TOMATO DEVILED EGGS

PREP 25 minutes

12   hard-boiled eggs
½   cup sun-dried tomatoes packed in oil, drained, patted dry, and finely chopped
⅓   cup mayonnaise
¼   cup plain Greek yogurt
1   Tbsp. white wine vinegar
1   Tbsp. Dijon mustard
¼   tsp. garlic powder
¼   tsp. salt
¼   tsp. black pepper
2   Tbsp. chopped fresh herbs, such as chives, oregano, basil, and/or dill

1. Peel eggs, halve lengthwise, and remove yolks. In a food processor combine yolks, all but 2 Tbsp. chopped tomatoes, the mayonnaise, yogurt, vinegar, mustard, garlic powder, salt, and pepper. Process until smooth. Spoon or pipe filling into egg whites.

ROASTED SWEET POTATO FRIES

2. Top with remaining tomatoes, herbs, and additional black pepper. Chill, covered, up to 24 hours before serving. Makes 24 servings.

PER SERVING *63 cal., 5 g fat (1 g sat. fat), 94 mg chol., 94 mg sodium, 1 g carb., 0 g fiber, 4 g pro.*

ONION-BLUE CHEESE DIP

START TO FINISH 35 minutes

2	Tbsp. olive oil
2	large sweet onions, halved and thinly slivered
16	oz. cremini mushrooms, chopped
1	8-oz. pkg. reduced-fat cream cheese (neufchatel), softened
⅔	cup crumbled blue cheese
½	cup fat-free milk
2	tsp. snipped fresh thyme or sage
¼	tsp. salt
¼	tsp. freshly ground black pepper

Pear slices, melba toast, and/or whole grain crackers

1. In a large nonstick skillet heat olive oil on medium; add onions. Cook, covered, 10 minutes, stirring occasionally. Add mushrooms. Cook, uncovered, 8 to 10 minutes or until mushrooms are tender and onion is golden brown, stirring occasionally.

2. Add cream cheese, blue cheese, milk, thyme, salt, and pepper to onion mixture. Cook and stir on low until mixture is melted. Serve warm with pear slices, melba toast, and/or whole grain crackers. Makes 16 servings.

PER SERVING *99 cal., 7 g fat (3 g sat. fat), 15 mg chol., 172 mg sodium, 6 g carb., 1 g fiber, 4 g pro.*

SUN-DRIED TOMATO DEVILED EGGS

ONION-BLUE CHEESE DIP

CARAMELIZED SPICY
ROASTED RED PEPPER
ARTICHOKE DIP

CARAMELIZED SPICY ROASTED RED PEPPER ARTICHOKE DIP

PREP 15 minutes
BAKE 30 minutes at 350°F
COOL 15 minutes

2 14-oz. cans artichoke hearts, rinsed and drained
1 8-oz. carton sour cream
2 Tbsp. all-purpose flour
1 Tbsp. harissa paste
¾ cup finely shredded Parmesan cheese
½ cup mayonnaise
½ cup bottled drained and chopped roasted red sweet peppers
¼ cup almonds, toasted and coarsely chopped (tip, page 22) Fresh mint leaves

1. Preheat oven to 350°F. Place artichoke hearts in a fine-mesh sieve or colander. To remove excess liquid, firmly press artichoke hearts with paper towels. Chop artichoke hearts.
2. In a large bowl stir together sour cream, flour, and harissa paste until combined. Stir in ½ cup of the cheese, mayonnaise, roasted peppers, and artichokes. Transfer to a 9-inch pie plate. Sprinkle with remaining ¼ cup cheese.
3. Bake, uncovered, 30 minutes or until edges are lightly browned and dip is hot in center. Cool 15 minutes. Top with almonds and mint. Makes 14 servings.
PER SERVING *134 cal., 11 g fat (3 g sat. fat), 16 mg chol., 267 mg sodium, 5 g carb., 1 g fiber, 3 g pro.*

OATMEAL CREAM PIE SIPPER

GINGER-PEAR CIDER

OATMEAL CREAM PIE SIPPER

PREP 15 minutes
SLOW COOK 4 hours (low)

4   cups half-and-half or light cream
4   cups oat milk or unsweetened almond milk
¾   cup packed brown sugar
1½ tsp. pumpkin pie spice
¼   cup butter, cut up
1   vanilla bean
4   egg yolks
1   to 2 Tbsp. Irish cream liqueur (optional)
4   3-inch oatmeal, sugar, or shortbread cookies, crumbled
1½ cups sweetened whipped cream

1. In a 3½- or 4-qt. slow cooker whisk together half-and-half, oat milk, brown sugar, and pumpkin pie spice. Whisk until sugar is dissolved. Add butter.

Using a small sharp knife, split vanilla bean in half lengthwise; scrape out the seeds. Add seeds and pod to cooker.
2. Cover and cook on low 4 to 5 hours, whisking once or twice, if possible.
3. Remove and discard vanilla bean pods. In a medium bowl whisk egg yolks. Gradually whisk about 2 cups hot liquid into yolks. Whisk egg yolk mixture into liquid in cooker until combined.
4. If desired, add Irish cream liqueur to each mug before adding the hot drink. Top servings with whipped cream and crumbled cookies. Makes 12 servings.
PER SERVING *336 cal., 22 g fat (12 g sat. fat), 122 mg chol., 137 mg sodium, 31 g carb., 1 g fiber, 5 g pro.*

GINGER-PEAR CIDER

PREP 10 minutes
SLOW COOK 3 hours (low)

2   qt. fresh apple cider
1   large Bosc pear, cored and cut into thin wedges
½   medium orange, sliced
1   3-inch cinnamon stick
1   1-inch piece fresh ginger, sliced
1½ tsp. vanilla
    Orange slices
    Bourbon, spiced rum, or applejack (optional)

1. Pour cider into a 4- to 6-qt. slow cooker. Add pear, orange slices, cinnamon, ginger, and vanilla. Cover and cook on low 3 to 4 hours.
2. Ladle into mugs to serve. Garnish with additional orange slices. If desired, add bourbon to each serving. Makes 12 servings.
PER SERVING *107 cal., 0 g fat, 0 mg chol., 17 mg sodium, 26 g carb., 1 g fiber, 0 g pro.*

CHOCOLATE CAKE
WITH MALT TOPPING

CHOCOLATE CAKE WITH MALT TOPPING

PREP 25 minutes
BAKE 17 minutes at 350°F
COOL 40 minutes
CHILL 3 hours

½ cup unsweetened cocoa powder
2 cups all-purpose flour
1 tsp. baking powder
½ tsp. baking soda
⅔ cup butter, softened
1¾ cups sugar
3 eggs
4 oz. unsweetened chocolate, melted and cooled
2 tsp. vanilla
1½ cups milk
1 recipe Chocolate Malt Frosting
2 cups malted milk balls or miniature malted milk balls

1. Preheat oven to 350°F. Grease three 8-inch square or 9-inch round baking pans. Lightly dust each pan with 1 tsp. of the cocoa powder; set pans aside. In a medium bowl stir together remaining cocoa powder, flour, baking powder, and baking soda.
2. In a large bowl beat butter with a mixer on medium to high 30 seconds. Add sugar; beat until combined. Add eggs, one at a time, beating 30 seconds after each addition. Beat in chocolate and vanilla. Alternately add flour mixture and milk to beaten mixture, beating on low until thoroughly combined. Spread batter in prepared pans.
3. Bake 17 to 20 minutes or until a toothpick inserted near centers comes out clean. Cool cakes in pans on wire racks 10 minutes. Remove cakes from pans. Cool completely on wire racks.
4. Fill and frost cake with Chocolate Malt Frosting, reserving some frosting for piping. Place reserved frosting in a decorating bag fitted with a medium round tip. Starting from the bottom, pipe zigzags on sides and top edge of cake. If desired, coarsely chop or halve some malted milk balls. Decorate cake with malted milk balls. Cover and chill until ready to serve. Cover and store any leftovers in refrigerator. Makes 20 servings.

Chocolate Malt Frosting In a medium saucepan heat 2 cups heavy cream over medium-high just until boiling. Remove from heat. Stir in ⅓ cup malted milk powder. Add two 11.5-oz. pkg. milk chocolate pieces (do not stir). Cover and let stand 5 minutes. Stir until smooth (mixture will be thin). Transfer to a large bowl. Cover and chill 3 hours or until frosting is thoroughly chilled. Set bowl of frosting in a larger bowl of ice water. Beat frosting with a mixer on medium 3 minutes or until fluffy and spreading consistency (frosting will turn light brown).
PER SERVING *540 cal., 32 g fat (17 g sat. fat), 83 mg chol., 263 mg sodium, 61 g carb., 1 g fiber, 8 g pro.*

APPLE-BROWN BUTTER BARS

PREP 20 minutes
BAKE 40 minutes at 350°F

Nonstick cooking spray
1½ cups plus 2 Tbsp. all-purpose flour
½ 8-oz. pkg. almond paste, crumbled
½ cup packed brown sugar
¼ cup almonds
½ cup cold butter, cut up
¼ cup butter
¼ tsp. ground cinnamon
¼ tsp. ground allspice
2 eggs, lightly beaten
⅔ cup granulated sugar
⅓ cup apple juice
2 Tbsp. heavy cream
2 to 3 medium apples (6 oz. each), such as Honeycrisp, Gala, and/or Granny Smith, cored, halved, and very thinly sliced
2 Tbsp. apple jelly (optional)
Sea salt flakes

1. Preheat oven to 350°F. Line a 9-inch square baking pan with foil; coat foil with nonstick cooking spray. In a food processor combine 1½ cups flour, almond paste, brown sugar, and almonds. Cover and pulse until finely chopped. Add ½ cup cold butter; cover and pulse until crumbly. Pat mixture into prepared pan. Bake 15 minutes or until edges are light brown.

2. Meanwhile, for spiced brown butter, heat ¼ cup butter in a small saucepan over medium-low 15 minutes or until brown. Remove from heat. Stir in cinnamon and allspice.

3. For filling, in a small bowl whisk together eggs, granulated sugar, apple juice, remaining 2 Tbsp. flour, and cream. Pour over hot crust. Bake 15 minutes. (Filling will not be completely set.) Arrange and overlap apple slices on filling. Brush with half the brown butter mixture. Bake 10 to 15 minutes or until apples are tender.

4. Cool on a wire rack. Drizzle with remaining brown butter. If desired, brush with apple jelly. Sprinkle with sea salt flakes. Makes 16 servings.

PER SERVING 257 cal., 13 g fat (6 g sat. fat), 48 mg chol., 118 mg sodium, 32 g carb., 1 g fiber, 3 g pro.

APPLE-BROWN BUTTER BARS

SALTED CHOCOLATE-
CARAMEL ROUNDS,
PAGE 154

CHEESY BRUSSELS
SPROUTS AND
CHORIZO BAKE,
PAGE 153

Weekend Houseguests

Add to the fun of the season by hosting holiday guests. Be
prepared with these easy recipes that fit into busy schedules.

PIMIENTO CHEESE DIP

PIMIENTO CHEESE DIP

PREP 15 minutes
CHILL 1 hour

2   cups smoked cheddar cheese
¾   cup mayonnaise
8   oz. softened cream cheese
1   tsp. freshly cracked black pepper
¼   tsp. kosher salt
     Pinch of cayenne pepper
4   oz. diced pimiento
     Crackers and crudites

1. In a food processor combine cheddar cheese, mayonnaise, cream cheese, black pepper, salt, and cayenne. Stir in pimiento. Transfer to a serving bowl. Cover and chill 1 hour. Serve with crackers and crudites. Makes 10 servings.
PER SERVING *243 cal., 24 g fat (9 g sat. fat), 42 mg chol., 330 mg sodium, 2 g carb., 0 g fiber, 7 g pro.*

BOURBON-BROWN SUGAR NUTS

PREP 20 minutes
COOK 15 minutes
COOL 25 minutes

½   cup packed brown sugar
3   Tbsp. bourbon
1   cup toasted whole almonds
½   tsp. kosher salt
½   tsp. freshly cracked black pepper
½   tsp. ground cinnamon
⅛   to ¼ tsp. cayenne pepper

1. Line a shallow baking pan with foil; grease foil.
2. In a medium saucepan combine brown sugar and bourbon. Bring to boiling over medium-high, stirring to dissolve sugar. Stir in almonds. Reduce heat to medium; cook 4 minutes or until syrup thickens slightly, stirring often. Reduce heat to medium-low. Stir in salt, black pepper, cinnamon, and cayenne (mixture will be foamy). Cook 7 minutes more or until syrup thickens and coats nuts, stirring frequently.
3. Spread nuts in a single layer in prepared pan. Cool completely. Break apart. Store in an airtight container up to 1 week. Makes 6 servings.
PER SERVING *225 cal., 12 g fat (1 g sat. fat), 0 mg chol., 99 mg sodium, 23 g carb., 3 g fiber, 5 g pro.*

BOURBON-BROWN
SUGAR NUTS

TURKEY-APPLE
GRILLED CHEESE
SANDWICHES

TURKEY-APPLE GRILLED CHEESE SANDWICHES

START TO FINISH 25 minutes

1   medium sweet onion, such as Vidalia or Maui Maui, cut into thin wedges
1   Tbsp. vegetable oil
2   Tbsp. apple jelly
8   slices country-style or whole grain bread
8   slices white cheddar or Gouda cheese
8   oz. deli-roasted turkey or chicken, sliced
1   medium Granny Smith apple, cored and thinly sliced
2   to 3 Tbsp. butter, softened

1. In a large skillet cook onion in hot oil over medium heat 8 to 10 minutes or until very tender and beginning to brown. Remove onion to a small bowl; stir in apple jelly. If desired, snip onions into smaller pieces.

2. Top half the bread slices with 1 slice of cheese, turkey, apple slices, onion mixture, and remaining cheese slice. Top with remaining bread slices.

3. Spread top slices of bread with half the butter. Heat an extra-large skillet over medium heat. Place sandwiches, buttered sides down, in skillet. Carefully spread unbuttered bread with remaining butter. Cook 4 to 6 minutes or until cheese is melted and bread is browned, turning once. Makes 4 servings.

PER SERVING *562 cal., 28 g fat (13 g sat. fat), 115 mg chol., 585 mg sodium, 43 g carb., 6 g fiber, 35 g pro.*

CHICKEN AND SPINACH DUMPLINGS

PREP 30 minutes
COOK 10 minutes

2   eggs, lightly beaten
2   cups packed fresh spinach, chopped
1   cup ricotta cheese
¾   cup all-purpose flour
½   cup finely shredded Asiago cheese (2 oz.)
1   tsp. lemon zest
1   32-oz. carton reduced-sodium chicken broth

1   Tbsp. fresh thyme leaves
¼   cup all-purpose flour
⅓   cup thinly sliced carrot
2   cups shredded or chopped cooked chicken

1. In a medium bowl combine the first six ingredients (through lemon zest). (Dough will be soft.) In a Dutch oven combine broth and thyme. Bring to boiling.

2. Place ¼ cup flour in a shallow dish. Using a teaspoon, scoop a portion of dough into flour. Gently roll dough to coat, forming an oval. Drop coated dough pieces, one-fourth at a time, into broth. Simmer 1 to 1½ minutes or until dumplings float, stirring once or twice to prevent dumplings from sticking together. Using a slotted spoon, remove dumplings from Dutch oven.

3. Add carrot to broth; cook 5 minutes or until soft. Return all dumplings to Dutch oven. Stir in chicken; heat through. Top servings with additional Asiago cheese, lemon zest, and/or thyme. Makes 4 servings.

PER SERVING *498 cal., 23 g fat (12 g sat. fat), 204 mg chol., 886 mg sodium, 29 g carb., 2 g fiber, 41 g pro.*

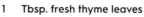

CHICKEN AND SPINACH DUMPLINGS

CAULIFLOWER TABBOULEH

PREP 20 minutes
STAND 1 hour

- 3 Tbsp. olive oil
- 1 1½-lb. head cauliflower, finely chopped (5 cups)
- 1½ tsp. kosher salt
- 1 Tbsp. lemon zest
- ¼ cup lemon juice
- ½ tsp. sugar
- ½ cup sliced green onions
- 1 cup chopped fresh herbs, such as mint, parsley, and/or dill weed
- 1 cup cherry tomatoes, halved
- ½ medium cucumber, seeded and chopped (1 cup)
- ½ cup sunflower kernels

1. Heat olive oil in an extra-large nonstick skillet over medium-high. Add cauliflower and 1 tsp. of the salt to skillet. Cook, stirring occasionally, 5 minutes or until crisp-tender. Spread cauliflower on a large baking sheet to cool.
2. In a large bowl stir together remaining salt, lemon zest, lemon juice, and sugar. Add cooled cauliflower, green onions, herbs, cherry tomatoes, and cucumber. Cover and let stand at room temperature 1 hour, stirring occasionally.
3. Just before serving, stir in sunflower kernels. Serve with lemon wedges and drizzle with additional olive oil if desired. Makes 4 servings.
PER SERVING *241 cal., 19 g fat (2 g sat. fat), 0 mg chol., 576 mg sodium, 16 g carb., 6 g fiber, 7 g pro.*

ROASTED STEAK WITH TOMATOES AND MUSHROOMS

START TO FINISH 30 minutes

- 1 8-oz. pkg. sliced fresh mushrooms
- 1 pint red and/or yellow cherry or grape tomatoes
- 3 Tbsp. olive oil
- 1 Tbsp. balsamic vinegar
- 3 cloves garlic, minced
- ¼ tsp. salt
- ¼ tsp. black pepper
- 2 to 3 beef shoulder petite tenders (about 1½ lb. total) or 1½ lb. boneless beef top sirloin, cut 1½ inches thick
- 1 Tbsp. Montreal steak seasoning
- 2 to 3 tsp. chopped fresh oregano Shaved Parmesan cheese

1. Preheat oven to 450°F. Line a 15×10-inch baking pan with foil. In the pan combine mushrooms, tomatoes, 1 Tbsp. of the olive oil, vinegar, garlic, salt, and pepper. Toss to combine. Spread in an even layer. Roast about 15 minutes or until tomatoes are softened and mushrooms are tender.
2. Meanwhile, sprinkle meat all over with steak seasoning. In a large oven-going skillet heat remaining 2 Tbsp. olive oil over medium-high. Add meat. Cook about 8 minutes or until well browned on all sides. Transfer skillet to oven. Roast 5 to 8 minutes or until medium-rare (145°F). Transfer meat to cutting board; cover with foil and let stand 5 minutes. Slice meat.
3. Add oregano to tomato mixture; toss to combine. Serve with sliced steak. Top with shaved Parmesan cheese and additional fresh oregano. Makes 4 servings.
PER SERVING *339 cal., 18 g fat (5 g sat. fat), 95 mg chol., 879 mg sodium, 5 g carb., 1 g fiber, 40 g pro.*

CAULIFLOWER TABBOULEH

ROASTED STEAK
WITH TOMATOES
AND MUSHROOMS

CHEESY BRUSSELS
SPROUTS AND
CHORIZO BAKE

CHEESY BRUSSELS SPROUTS AND CHORIZO BAKE

PREP 20 minutes
BAKE 30 minutes at 400°F
STAND 15 minutes

1   lb. small Brussels sprouts, trimmed and quartered (2¾ cups)
8   oz. whole tiny new potatoes, thinly sliced (1¾ cups)
3   oz. cooked smoked chorizo sausage, thinly sliced
1   shallot, finely chopped
1   egg, lightly beaten
2   cups heavy cream
½   tsp. kosher salt
4   oz. Manchego cheese or Parmesan cheese, shredded (1 cup)

1. Preheat oven to 400°F. Divide Brussels sprouts, potatoes, chorizo, and shallot among four 12- to 14-oz. baking dishes.
2. In a medium bowl combine egg, cream, and salt; divide among dishes. Top each with cheese. Place baking dishes in a 15×10-inch baking pan. Bake 30 minutes or until potatoes and sprouts are tender. Let stand 15 minutes before serving. Makes 4 servings.
PER SERVING *753 cal., 66 g fat (40 g sat. fat), 258 mg chol., 963 mg sodium, 22 g carb., 5 g fiber, 21 g pro.*

SPICY SCALLOPED SWEET POTATOES

PREP 30 minutes
BAKE 1 hour 10 minutes at 375°F
STAND 5 minutes

1   Tbsp. olive oil
¾   cup chopped red sweet pepper
½   cup chopped onion
3   cloves garlic, thinly sliced
1   Tbsp. finely chopped canned chipotle pepper in adobo sauce
1   tsp. salt
3   lb. sweet potatoes, peeled and very thinly sliced
1   cup heavy cream
¾   cup chicken broth
¾   cup shredded sharp cheddar cheese (3 oz.)

SPICY SCALLOPED SWEET POTATOES

1. Preheat oven to 375°F. In a 12-inch cast-iron skillet heat oil over medium-high. Add sweet pepper and onion; cook 4 to 5 minutes or just until tender, stirring occasionally. Add garlic; cook and stir 1 minute more. Remove from heat. Stir in chipotle pepper and salt. Transfer mixture to a small bowl.
2. Arrange sweet potatoes and pepper mixture in the same skillet, alternating layers. In a small bowl stir together cream and broth; pour over potato mixture. Sprinkle with cheese.
3. Transfer skillet to oven and bake, covered, 40 minutes. Bake, uncovered, 30 minutes more or until potatoes are tender and top is light brown. Let stand 5 to 10 minutes before serving. Makes 8 servings.
PER SERVING *319 cal., 17 g fat (9 g sat. fat), 53 mg chol., 552 mg sodium, 38 g carb., 6 g fiber, 6 g pro.*

PEANUT BUTTER CHIP-OATMEAL CAKE

SALTED CHOCOLATE-CARAMEL ROUNDS

PREP 30 minutes
BAKE 8 minutes per batch at 375°F

2¾ cups all-purpose flour
¾ cup unsweetened cocoa powder
1 tsp. baking soda
¼ tsp. salt
1 cup butter, softened
1 cup granulated sugar
1 cup packed brown sugar
2 eggs
2 tsp. vanilla
36 milk chocolate-covered round caramels
12 vanilla caramels, unwrapped
1 Tbsp. heavy cream, half-and-half, or light cream
Coarse salt

1. In a medium bowl stir together flour, cocoa powder, baking soda, and salt; set aside.
2. In a large bowl beat butter with a mixer on medium to high 30 seconds. Add granulated and brown sugar. Beat until combined, scraping sides of bowl occasionally. Beat in eggs and vanilla until combined. Beat in as much of the flour mixture as you can with the mixer. Stir in any remaining flour mixture. If necessary, cover and chill 1 hour or until dough is easy to handle.
3. Preheat oven to 375°F. Shape dough into 1½-inch balls. Press a chocolate-covered caramel into each ball and shape dough around caramel to enclose. Place cookies 2 inches apart on an ungreased cookie sheet.
4. Bake 8 to 10 minutes or until edges are firm. Transfer cookies to a wire rack; cool completely.
5. For caramel drizzle, in a small saucepan combine vanilla caramels and cream. Heat over medium-low until caramels melt and mixture is smooth. Drizzle melted caramel over cookies then sprinkle with coarse salt. Let stand until set. Makes 8 servings.
PER SERVING *177 cal., 8 g fat (5 g sat. fat), 27 mg chol., 140 mg sodium, 26 g carb., 1 g fiber, 2 g pro.*

PEANUT BUTTER CHIP-OATMEAL CAKE

PREP 25 minutes
BAKE 35 minutes at 350°F

1¾ cups boiling water
1 cup quick-cooking rolled oats
1 cup granulated sugar
1 cup packed brown sugar
½ cup butter, cut up and softened
2 eggs
1¾ cups all-purpose flour
1 tsp. baking soda
1 tsp. ground cinnamon
½ tsp. salt
1 10-oz. pkg. peanut butter-flavor pieces
¾ cup chopped pecans
Peanut butter and/or grape jelly, warmed (optional)

1. Preheat oven to 350°F. In a large bowl combine boiling water and oats; let stand 10 minutes. Meanwhile, grease a 13×9-inch baking pan.
2. Add both sugars and butter to oats mixture, stirring until butter is melted. Stir in eggs until combined. Stir in flour, baking soda, cinnamon, and salt. Stir in 1 cup of the peanut butter pieces.
3. Spread batter in prepared pan. Sprinkle with pecans and remaining peanut butter pieces. Bake 35 minutes or until a toothpick comes out clean. Cool in pan on a wire rack. If desired, drizzle with warmed peanut butter and/or jelly. Makes 20 servings.
PER SERVING *274 cal., 13 g fat (7 g sat. fat), 31 mg chol., 196 mg sodium, 36 g carb., 2 g fiber, 6 g pro.*

SALTED CHOCOLATE-
CARAMEL ROUNDS

Index